Friendship
& other essays

Friendship
& other essays

Ralph Waldo Emerson

This edition published in 2019 by Arcturus Publishing Limited
26/27 Bickels Yard, 151–153 Bermondsey Street,
London SE1 3HA

AD006325US

Printed in the UK

Contents

Introduction

Ralph Waldo Emerson was born in Boston, Massachusetts on May 25, 1803. His father died when Emerson was only eight years old. He began studying at Harvard College when just 14 and graduated four years later. While Emerson was only a passable student, he had already begun to develop a passion for literature and even served as "Class Poet."

After graduation, he established his own school in Chelmsford, Massachussetts, and assisted his brother in running a school for young girls in their mother's house. He continued to teach until 1825, when he made the decision to attend Harvard Divinity School.

In 1827, Emerson met his first wife, Ellen Louisa Tucker in New Hampshire. The pair soon married and moved to Boston, where Emerson became an ordained pastor for Boston's Second Church. Ellen died in 1831, leading to a crisis of faith for Emerson.

In 1833, Emerson traveled to Europe and was mesmerized by the *Jardin des Plantes*, a botanical garden in France. Upon his return to the US, Emerson spoke

about his experiences abroad in his first lecture, sharing ideas that he later developed into his famous essay "Nature." In 1835, Emerson married his second wife, Lydia Jackson, and the pair later had four children.

With the publication of "Nature" in 1836, Emerson set forth the ideals of transcendentalism, a literary movement which focused on the knowledge and spirituality that people can gain from immersing themselves in nature. Nineteenth-century transcendentalists believed that humanity is inherently good, but that it is corrupted by society and its institutions, and that people should learn to be independent in order to become their best selves. Along with a number of like-minded individuals, Emerson established the Transcendental Club in 1836. Following on from the success of "Nature," Emerson went on to publish two collections of his essays, in 1841 and 1844, which outlined the key principles of his philosophy.

Emerson gave lectures and published many more essays before his death in 1882. While his beliefs were sometimes controversial, he had an incredible impact on the literary landscape of the nineteenth century. Transcendentalism was a defining aspect of the Romantic movement in America, and Emerson's work had a profound effect on many of the writers who followed him.

Friendship

A RUDDY drop of manly blood
The surging sea outweighs;
The world uncertain comes and goes,
The lover rooted stays.
I fancied he was fled,
And, after many a year,
Glowed unexhausted kindliness
Like daily sunrise there.
My careful heart was free again,—
O friend, my bosom said,
Through thee alone the sky is arched,
Through thee the rose is red,
All things through thee take nobler form
And look beyond the earth,
The mill-round of our fate appears
A sun-path in thy worth.
Me too thy nobleness has taught
To master my despair;
The fountains of my hidden life
Are through thy friendship fair.

9

We have a great deal more kindness than is ever spoken. Maugre all the selfishness that chills like east winds the world, the whole human family is bathed with an element of love like a fine ether. How many persons we meet in houses, whom we scarcely speak to, whom yet we honor, and who honor us! How many we see in the street, or sit with in church, whom, though silently, we warmly rejoice to be with! Read the language of these wandering eye-beams. The heart knoweth.

The effect of the indulgence of this human affection is a certain cordial exhilaration. In poetry and in common speech the emotions of benevolence and complacency which are felt towards others are likened to the material effects of fire; so swift, or much more swift, more active, more cheering, are these fine inward irradiations. From the highest degree of passionate love to the lowest degree of good-will, they make the sweetness of life.

Our intellectual and active powers increase with our affection. The scholar sits down to write, and all his years of meditation do not furnish him with one good thought or happy expression; but it is necessary to write a letter to a friend,—and forthwith troops of gentle thoughts invest themselves, on every hand, with chosen words. See, in any house where virtue and self-respect abide, the palpitation which the approach of a stranger causes. A commended stranger is expected and

announced, and an uneasiness betwixt pleasure and pain invades all the hearts of a household. His arrival almost brings fear to the good hearts that would welcome him. The house is dusted, all things fly into their places, the old coat is exchanged for the new, and they must get up a dinner if they can. Of a commended stranger, only the good report is told by others, only the good and new is heard by us. He stands to us for humanity. He is what we wish. Having imagined and invested him, we ask how we should stand related in conversation and action with such a man, and are uneasy with fear. The same idea exalts conversation with him. We talk better than we are wont. We have the nimblest fancy, a richer memory, and our dumb devil has taken leave for the time. For long hours we can continue a series of sincere, graceful, rich communications, drawn from the oldest, secretest experience, so that they who sit by, of our own kinsfolk and acquaintance, shall feel a lively surprise at our unusual powers. But as soon as the stranger begins to intrude his partialities, his definitions, his defects into the conversation, it is all over. He has heard the first, the last and best he will ever hear from us. He is no stranger now. Vulgarity, ignorance, misapprehension are old acquaintances. Now, when he comes, he may get the order, the dress and the dinner,—but the throbbing of the heart and the communications of the soul, no more.

What is so pleasant as these jets of affection which make a young world for me again? What so delicious as a just and firm encounter of two, in a thought, in a feeling? How beautiful, on their approach to this beating heart, the steps and forms of the gifted and the true! The moment we indulge our affections, the earth is metamorphosed; there is no winter and no night; all tragedies, all ennuis vanish,—all duties even; nothing fills the proceeding eternity but the forms all radiant of beloved persons. Let the soul be assured that somewhere in the universe it should rejoin its friend, and it would be content and cheerful alone for a thousand years.

I awoke this morning with devout thanksgiving for my friends, the old and the new. Shall I not call God the Beautiful, who daily showeth himself so to me in his gifts? I chide society, I embrace solitude, and yet I am not so ungrateful as not to see the wise, the lovely and the noble-minded, as from time to time they pass my gate. Who hears me, who understands me, becomes mine,—a possession for all time. Nor is Nature so poor but she gives me this joy several times, and thus we weave social threads of our own, a new web of relations; and, as many thoughts in succession substantiate themselves, we shall by and by stand in a new world of our own creation, and no longer strangers and pilgrims in a traditionary globe. My friends have come to me unsought. The great God gave them to me. By oldest

right, by the divine affinity of virtue with itself, I find them, or rather not I, but the Deity in me and in them derides and cancels the thick walls of individual character, relation, age, sex, circumstance, at which he usually connives, and now makes many one. High thanks I owe you, excellent lovers, who carry out the world for me to new and noble depths, and enlarge the meaning of all my thoughts. These are new poetry of the first Bard,—poetry without stop,—hymn, ode and epic, poetry still flowing, Apollo and the Muses chanting still. Will these too separate themselves from me again, or some of them? I know not, but I fear it not; for my relation to them is so pure that we hold by simple affinity, and the Genius of my life being thus social, the same affinity will exert its energy on whomsoever is as noble as these men and women, wherever I may be.

I confess to an extreme tenderness of nature on this point. It is almost dangerous to me to "crush the sweet poison of misused wine" of the affections. A new person is to me a great event and hinders me from sleep. I have often had fine fancies about persons which have given me delicious hours; but the joy ends in the day; it yields no fruit. Thought is not born of it; my action is very little modified. I must feel pride in my friend's accomplishments as if they were mine, and a property in his virtues. I feel as warmly when he is praised, as the lover when he hears applause of his engaged maiden. We

over-estimate the conscience of our friend. His goodness seems better than our goodness, his nature finer, his temptations less. Every thing that is his,—his name, his form, his dress, books and instruments,—fancy enhances. Our own thought sounds new and larger from his mouth.

Yet the systole and diastole of the heart are not without their analogy in the ebb and flow of love. Friendship, like the immortality of the soul, is too good to be believed. The lover, beholding his maiden, half knows that she is not verily that which he worships; and in the golden hour of friendship we are surprised with shades of suspicion and unbelief. We doubt that we bestow on our hero the virtues in which he shines, and afterwards worship the form to which we have ascribed this divine inhabitation. In strictness, the soul does not respect men as it respects itself. In strict science all persons underlie the same condition of an infinite remoteness. Shall we fear to cool our love by mining for the metaphysical foundation of this Elysian temple? Shall I not be as real as the things I see? If I am, I shall not fear to know them for what they are. Their essence is not less beautiful than their appearance, though it needs finer organs for its apprehension. The root of the plant is not unsightly to science, though for chaplets and festoons we cut the stem short. And I must hazard the production of the bald fact amidst these pleasing

reveries, though it should prove an Egyptian skull at our banquet. A man who stands united with his thought conceives magnificently of himself. He is conscious of a universal success, even though bought by uniform particular failures. No advantages, no powers, no gold or force, can be any match for him. I cannot choose but rely on my own poverty more than on your wealth. I cannot make your consciousness tantamount to mine. Only the star dazzles; the planet has a faint, moonlike ray. I hear what you say of the admirable parts and tried temper of the party you praise, but I see well that, for all his purple cloaks, I shall not like him, unless he is at least a poor Greek like me. I cannot deny it, O friend, that the vast shadow of the Phenomenal includes thee also in its pied and painted immensity,—thee also, compared with whom all else is shadow. Thou art not Being, as Truth is, as Justice is,—thou art not my soul, but a picture and effigy of that. Thou hast come to me lately, and already thou art seizing thy hat and cloak. Is it not that the soul puts forth friends as the tree puts forth leaves, and presently, by the germination of new buds, extrudes the old leaf? The law of nature is alternation for evermore. Each electrical state superinduces the opposite. The soul environs itself with friends that it may enter into a grander self-acquaintance or solitude; and it goes alone for a season that it may exalt its conversation or society. This method betrays itself along

the whole history of our personal relations. The instinct of affection revives the hope of union with our mates, and the returning sense of insulation recalls us from the chase. Thus every man passes his life in the search after friendship, and if he should record his true sentiment, he might write a letter like this to each new candidate for his love:—

DEAR FRIEND,

If I was sure of thee, sure of thy capacity, sure to match my mood with thine, I should never think again of trifles in relation to thy comings and goings. I am not very wise; my moods are quite attainable, and I respect thy genius; it is to me as yet unfathomed; yet dare I not presume in thee a perfect intelligence of me, and so thou art to me a delicious torment. Thine ever, or never.

Yet these uneasy pleasures and fine pains are for curiosity and not for life. They are not to be indulged. This is to weave cobweb, and not cloth. Our friendships hurry to short and poor conclusions, because we have made them a texture of wine and dreams, instead of the tough fibre of the human heart. The laws of friendship are austere and eternal, of one web with the

laws of nature and of morals. But we have aimed at a swift and petty benefit, to suck a sudden sweetness. We snatch at the slowest fruit in the whole garden of God, which many summers and many winters must ripen. We seek our friend not sacredly, but with an adulterate passion which would appropriate him to ourselves. In vain. We are armed all over with subtle antagonisms, which, as soon as we meet, begin to play, and translate all poetry into stale prose. Almost all people descend to meet. All association must be a compromise, and, what is worst, the very flower and aroma of the flower of each of the beautiful natures disappears as they approach each other. What a perpetual disappointment is actual society, even of the virtuous and gifted! After interviews have been compassed with long foresight we must be tormented presently by baffled blows, by sudden, unseasonable apathies, by epilepsies of wit and of animal spirits, in the heyday of friendship and thought. Our faculties do not play us true, and both parties are relieved by solitude.

I ought to be equal to every relation. It makes no difference how many friends I have and what content I can find in conversing with each, if there be one to whom I am not equal. If I have shrunk unequal from one contest, the joy I find in all the rest becomes mean and cowardly. I should hate myself, if then I made my other friends my asylum:—

"The valiant warrior famousèd for fight,
After a hundred victories, once foiled,
Is from the book of honor razèd quite
And all the rest forgot for which he toiled."

Our impatience is thus sharply rebuked. Bashfulness and apathy are a tough husk in which a delicate organization is protected from premature ripening. It would be lost if it knew itself before any of the best souls were yet ripe enough to know and own it. Respect the *naturlangsamkeit* which hardens the ruby in a million years, and works in duration in which Alps and Andes come and go as rainbows. The good spirit of our life has no heaven which is the price of rashness. Love, which is the essence of God, is not for levity, but for the total worth of man. Let us not have this childish luxury in our regards, but the austerest worth; let us approach our friend with an audacious trust in the truth of his heart, in the breadth, impossible to be overturned, of his foundations.

The attractions of this subject are not to be resisted, and I leave, for the time, all account of subordinate social benefit, to speak of that select and sacred relation which is a kind of absolute, and which even leaves the language of love suspicious and common, so much is this purer, and nothing is so much divine.

I do not wish to treat friendships daintily, but with roughest courage. When they are real, they are not glass

threads or frostwork, but the solidest thing we know. For now, after so many ages of experience, what do we know of nature or of ourselves? Not one step has man taken toward the solution of the problem of his destiny. In one condemnation of folly stand the whole universe of men. But the sweet sincerity of joy and peace which I draw from this alliance with my brother's soul is the nut itself whereof all nature and all thought is but the husk and shell. Happy is the house that shelters a friend! It might well be built, like a festal bower or arch, to entertain him a single day. Happier, if he know the solemnity of that relation and honor its law! He who offers himself a candidate for that covenant comes up, like an Olympian, to the great games where the firstborn of the world are the competitors. He proposes himself for contests where Time, Want, Danger, are in the lists, and he alone is victor who has truth enough in his constitution to preserve the delicacy of his beauty from the wear and tear of all these. The gifts of fortune may be present or absent, but all the speed in that contest depends on intrinsic nobleness and the contempt of trifles. There are two elements that go to the composition of friendship, each so sovereign that I can detect no superiority in either, no reason why either should be first named. One is truth. A friend is a person with whom I may be sincere. Before him I may think aloud. I am arrived at last in the presence of a man so real and

equal that I may drop even those undermost garments of dissimulation, courtesy, and second thought, which men never put off, and may deal with him with the simplicity and wholeness with which one chemical atom meets another. Sincerity is the luxury allowed, like diadems and authority, only to the highest rank; *that* being permitted to speak truth, as having none above it to court or conform unto. Every man alone is sincere. At the entrance of a second person, hypocrisy begins. We parry and fend the approach of our fellow-man by compliments, by gossip, by amusements, by affairs. We cover up our thought from him under a hundred folds. I knew a man who under a certain religious frenzy cast off this drapery, and omitting all compliment and commonplace, spoke to the conscience of every person he encountered, and that with great insight and beauty. At first he was resisted, and all men agreed he was mad. But persisting—as indeed he could not help doing—for some time in this course, he attained to the advantage of bringing every man of his acquaintance into true relations with him. No man would think of speaking falsely with him, or of putting him off with any chat of markets or reading-rooms. But every man was constrained by so much sincerity to the like plain dealing, and what love of nature, what poetry, what symbol of truth he had, he did certainly show him. But to most of us society shows not its face and eye, but its side and its back. To

stand in true relations with men in a false age is worth a fit of insanity, is it not? We can seldom go erect. Almost every man we meet requires some civility—requires to be humored; he has some fame, some talent, some whim of religion or philanthropy in his head that is not to be questioned, and which spoils all conversation with him. But a friend is a sane man who exercises not my ingenuity, but me. My friend gives me entertainment without requiring any stipulation on my part. A friend therefore is a sort of paradox in nature. I who alone am, I who see nothing in nature whose existence I can affirm with equal evidence to my own, behold now the semblance of my being, in all its height, variety and curiosity, reiterated in a foreign form; so that a friend may well be reckoned the masterpiece of nature.

The other element of friendship is tenderness. We are holden to men by every sort of tie, by blood, by pride, by fear, by hope, by lucre, by lust, by hate, by admiration, by every circumstance and badge and trifle,—but we can scarce believe that so much character can subsist in another as to draw us by love. Can another be so blessed and we so pure that we can offer him tenderness? When a man becomes dear to me I have touched the goal of fortune. I find very little written directly to the heart of this matter in books. And yet I have one text which I cannot choose but remember. My author says,—"I offer myself faintly and bluntly to those

whose I effectually am, and tender myself least to him to whom I am the most devoted." I wish that friendship should have feet, as well as eyes and eloquence. It must plant itself on the ground, before it vaults over the moon. I wish it to be a little of citizen, before it is quite a cherub. We chide the citizen because he makes love a commodity. It is an exchange of gifts, of useful loans; it is good neighborhood; it watches with the sick; it holds the pall at the funeral; and quite loses sight of the delicacies and nobility of the relation. But though we cannot find the god under this disguise of a sutler, yet on the other hand we cannot forgive the poet if he spins his thread too fine and does not substantiate his romance by the municipal virtues of justice, punctuality, fidelity and pity. I hate the prostitution of the name of friendship to signify modish and worldly alliances. I much prefer the company of ploughboys and tin-peddlers to the silken and perfumed amity which celebrates its days of encounter by a frivolous display, by rides in a curricle and dinners at the best taverns. The end of friendship is a commerce the most strict and homely that can be joined; more strict than any of which we have experience. It is for aid and comfort through all the relations and passages of life and death. It is fit for serene days and graceful gifts and country rambles, but also for rough roads and hard fare, shipwreck, poverty and persecution. It keeps company

with the sallies of the wit and the trances of religion. We are to dignify to each other the daily needs and offices of man's life, and embellish it by courage, wisdom and unity. It should never fall into something usual and settled, but should be alert and inventive and add rhyme and reason to what was drudgery.

Friendship may be said to require natures so rare and costly, each so well tempered and so happily adapted, and withal so circumstanced (for even in that particular, a poet says, love demands that the parties be altogether paired), that its satisfaction can very seldom be assured. It cannot subsist in its perfection, say some of those who are learned in this warm lore of the heart, betwixt more than two. I am not quite so strict in my terms, perhaps because I have never known so high a fellowship as others. I please my imagination more with a circle of godlike men and women variously related to each other and between whom subsists a lofty intelligence. But I find this law of *one to one* peremptory for conversation, which is the practice and consummation of friendship. Do not mix waters too much. The best mix as ill as good and bad. You shall have very useful and cheering discourse at several times with two several men, but let all three of you come together and you shall not have one new and hearty word. Two may talk and one may hear, but three cannot take part in a conversation of the most sincere and searching sort. In

good company there is never such discourse between two, across the table, as takes place when you leave them alone. In good company the individuals merge their egotism into a social soul exactly co-extensive with the several consciousnesses there present. No partialities of friend to friend, no fondnesses of brother to sister, of wife to husband, are there pertinent, but quite otherwise. Only he may then speak who can sail on the common thought of the party, and not poorly limited to his own. Now this convention, which good sense demands, destroys the high freedom of great conversation, which requires an absolute running of two souls into one.

No two men but being left alone with each other enter into simpler relations. Yet it is affinity that determines *which* two shall converse. Unrelated men give little joy to each other, will never suspect the latent powers of each. We talk sometimes of a great talent for conversation, as if it were a permanent property in some individuals. Conversation is an evanescent relation,—no more. A man is reputed to have thought and eloquence; he cannot, for all that, say a word to his cousin or his uncle. They accuse his silence with as much reason as they would blame the insignificance of a dial in the shade. In the sun it will mark the hour. Among those who enjoy his thought he will regain his tongue.

Friendship requires that rare mean betwixt likeness and unlikeness that piques each with the presence of

power and of consent in the other party. Let me be alone to the end of the world, rather than that my friend should overstep, by a word or a look, his real sympathy. I am equally balked by antagonism and by compliance. Let him not cease an instant to be himself. The only joy I have in his being mine, is that the *not mine* is *mine*. I hate, where I looked for a manly furtherance or at least a manly resistance, to find a mush of concession. Better be a nettle in the side of your friend than his echo. The condition which high friendship demands is ability to do without it. That high office requires great and sublime parts. There must be very two, before there can be very one. Let it be an alliance of two large, formidable natures, mutually beheld, mutually feared, before yet they recognize the deep identity which, beneath these disparities, unites them.

He only is fit for this society who is magnanimous; who is sure that greatness and goodness are always economy; who is not swift to intermeddle with his fortunes. Let him not intermeddle with this. Leave to the diamond its ages to grow, nor expect to accelerate the births of the eternal. Friendship demands a religious treatment. We talk of choosing our friends, but friends are self-elected. Reverence is a great part of it. Treat your friend as a spectacle. Of course he has merits that are not yours, and that you cannot honor if you must needs hold him close to your person. Stand aside; give

those merits room; let them mount and expand. Are you the friend of your friend's buttons, or of his thought? To a great heart he will still be a stranger in a thousand particulars, that he may come near in the holiest ground. Leave it to girls and boys to regard a friend as property, and to suck a short and all-confounding pleasure, instead of the noblest benefit.

Let us buy our entrance to this guild by a long probation. Why should we desecrate noble and beautiful souls by intruding on them? Why insist on rash personal relations with your friend? Why go to his house, or know his mother and brother and sisters? Why be visited by him at your own? Are these things material to our covenant? Leave this touching and clawing. Let him be to me a spirit. A message, a thought, a sincerity, a glance from him, I want, but not news, nor pottage. I can get politics and chat and neighborly conveniences from cheaper companions. Should not the society of my friend be to me poetic, pure, universal and great as nature itself? Ought I to feel that our tie is profane in comparison with yonder bar of cloud that sleeps on the horizon, or that clump of waving grass that divides the brook? Let us not vilify, but raise it to that standard. That great defying eye, that scornful beauty of his mien and action, do not pique yourself on reducing, but rather fortify and enhance. Worship his superiorities; wish him not less by a thought, but hoard and tell them all. Guard

him as thy counterpart. Let him be to thee for ever a sort of beautiful enemy, untamable, devoutly revered, and not a trivial conveniency to be soon outgrown and cast aside. The hues of the opal, the light of the diamond, are not to be seen if the eye is too near. To my friend I write a letter and from him I receive a letter. That seems to you a little. It suffices me. It is a spiritual gift, worthy of him to give and of me to receive. It profanes nobody. In these warm lines the heart will trust itself, as it will not to the tongue, and pour out the prophecy of a godlier existence than all the annals of heroism have yet made good.

Respect so far the holy laws of this fellowship as not to prejudice its perfect flower by your impatience for its opening. We must be our own before we can be another's. There is at least this satisfaction in crime, according to the Latin proverb;—you can speak to your accomplice on even terms. *Crimen quos inquinat, æquat.* To those whom we admire and love, at first we cannot. Yet the least defect of self-possession vitiates, in my judgment, the entire relation. There can never be deep peace between two spirits, never mutual respect, until in their dialogue each stands for the whole world.

What is so great as friendship, let us carry with what grandeur of spirit we can. Let us be silent,—so we may hear the whisper of the gods. Let us not interfere. Who set you to cast about what you should say to the select souls, or how to say any thing to such? No matter how ingenious, no matter how graceful and bland. There are innumerable degrees of folly and wisdom, and for you to say aught is to be frivolous. Wait, and thy heart shall speak. Wait until the necessary and everlasting overpowers you, until day and night avail themselves of your lips. The only reward of virtue is virtue; the only way to have a friend is to be one. You shall not come nearer a man by getting into his house. If unlike, his soul only flees the faster from you, and you shall never catch a true glance of his eye. We see the noble afar off and they repel us; why should we intrude? Late,— very late,—we perceive that no arrangements, no introductions, no consuetudes or habits of society would be of any avail to establish us in such relations with them as we desire,—but solely the uprise of nature in us to the same degree it is in them; then shall we meet as water with water; and if we should not meet them then, we shall not want them, for we are already they. In the last analysis, love is only the reflection of a man's own worthiness from other men. Men have sometimes exchanged names with their friends, as if they would signify that in their friend each loved his own soul.

The higher the style we demand of friendship, of course the less easy to establish it with flesh and blood. We walk alone in the world. Friends such as we desire are dreams and fables. But a sublime hope cheers ever

the faithful heart, that elsewhere, in other regions of the universal power, souls are now acting, enduring and daring, which can love us and which we can love. We may congratulate ourselves that the period of nonage, of follies, of blunders and of shame, is passed in solitude, and when we are finished men we shall grasp heroic hands in heroic hands. Only be admonished by what you already see, not to strike leagues of friendship with cheap persons, where no friendship can be. Our impatience betrays us into rash and foolish alliances which no god attends. By persisting in your path, though you forfeit the little you gain the great. You demonstrate yourself, so as to put yourself out of the reach of false relations, and you draw to you the first-born of the world,—those rare pilgrims whereof only one or two wander in nature at once, and before whom the vulgar great show as spectres and shadows merely.

It is foolish to be afraid of making our ties too spiritual, as if so we could lose any genuine love. Whatever correction of our popular views we make from insight, nature will be sure to bear us out in, and though it seem to rob us of some joy, will repay us with a greater. Let us feel if we will the absolute insulation of man. We are sure that we have all in us. We go to Europe, or we pursue persons, or we read books, in the instinctive faith that these will call it out and reveal us to ourselves. Beggars all. The persons are such as we;

the Europe, an old faded garment of dead persons; the books, their ghosts. Let us drop this idolatry. Let us give over this mendicancy. Let us even bid our dearest friends farewell, and defy them, saying 'Who are you? Unhand me: I will be dependent no more.' Ah! seest thou not, O brother, that thus we part only to meet again on a higher platform, and only be more each other's because we are more our own? A friend is Janus-faced; he looks to the past and the future. He is the child of all my foregoing hours, the prophet of those to come, and the harbinger of a greater friend.

I do then with my friends as I do with my books. I would have them where I can find them, but I seldom use them. We must have society on our own terms, and admit or exclude it on the slightest cause. I cannot afford to speak much with my friend. If he is great he makes me so great that I cannot descend to converse. In the great days, presentiments hover before me in the firmament. I ought then to dedicate myself to them. I go in that I may seize them, I go out that I may seize them. I fear only that I may lose them receding into the sky in which now they are only a patch of brighter light. Then, though I prize my friends, I cannot afford to talk with them and study their visions, lest I lose my own. It would indeed give me a certain household joy to quit this lofty seeking, this spiritual astronomy or search of stars, and come down to warm sympathies

with you; but then I know well I shall mourn always the vanishing of my mighty gods. It is true, next week I shall have languid moods, when I can well afford to occupy myself with foreign objects; then I shall regret the lost literature of your mind, and wish you were by my side again. But if you come, perhaps you will fill my mind only with new visions; not with yourself but with your lustres, and I shall not be able any more than now to converse with you. So I will owe to my friends this evanescent intercourse. I will receive from them not what they have but what they are. They shall give me that which properly they cannot give, but which emanates from them. But they shall not hold me by any relations less subtle and pure. We will meet as though we met not, and part as though we parted not.

It has seemed to me lately more possible than I knew, to carry a friendship greatly, on one side, without due correspondence on the other. Why should I cumber myself with regrets that the receiver is not capacious? It never troubles the sun that some of his rays fall wide and vain into ungrateful space, and only a small part on the reflecting planet. Let your greatness educate the crude and cold companion. If he is unequal, he will presently pass away; but thou art enlarged by thy own shining, and no longer a mate for frogs and worms, dost soar and burn with the gods of the empyrean. It is thought a disgrace to love unrequited. But the great

will see that true love cannot be unrequited. True love transcends the unworthy object and dwells and broods on the eternal, and when the poor interposed mask crumbles, it is not sad, but feels rid of so much earth and feels its independency the surer. Yet these things may hardly be said without a sort of treachery to the relation. The essence of friendship is entireness, a total magnanimity and trust. It must not surmise or provide for infirmity. It treats its object as a god, that it may deify both.

Love

"I was as a gem concealed;
Me my burning ray revealed."
Koran

Every promise of the soul has innumerable fulfil-ments; each often. Nature, uncontainable, flowing, forelooking, in the first sentiment of kindness anticipates already a benevolence which shall lose all particular regards in its general light. The introduction to this felicity is in a private and tender relation of one to one, which is the enchantment of human life; which, like a certain divine rage and enthusiasm, seizes on man at one period, and works a revolution in his mind and body; unites him to his race, pledges him to the domestic and civic relations, carries him with new sympathy into nature, enhances the power of the senses, opens the imagination, adds to his character heroic and sacred attributes, establishes marriage, and gives permanence to human society.

The natural association of the sentiment of love with the heyday of the blood seems to require, that in order to portray it in vivid tints, which every youth and maid should confess to be true to their throbbing experience, one must not be too old. The delicious fancies of youth reject the least savour of a mature philosophy, as chilling with age and pedantry their purple bloom. And, therefore, I know I incur the imputation of unnecessary hardness and stoicism from those who compose the Court and Parliament of Love. But from these formidable censors I shall appeal to my seniors. For it is to be considered that this passion of which we speak, though it begin with the young, yet forsakes not the old, or rather suffers no one who is truly its servant to grow old, but makes the aged participators of it, not less than the tender maiden, though in a different and nobler sort. For it is a fire that, kindling its first embers in the narrow nook of a private bosom, caught from a wandering spark out of another private heart, glows and enlarges until it warms and beams upon multitudes of men and women, upon the universal heart of all, and so lights up the whole world and all nature with its generous flames. It matters not, therefore, whether we attempt to describe the passion at twenty, at thirty, or at eighty years. He who paints it at the first period will lose some of its later, he who paints it at the last, some of its earlier traits. Only it is to be hoped that, by

patience and the Muses' aid, we may attain to that inward view of the law, which shall describe a truth ever young and beautiful, so central that it shall commend itself to the eye, at whatever angle beholden.

And the first condition is, that we must leave a too close and lingering adherence to facts, and study the sentiment as it appeared in hope and not in history. For each man sees his own life defaced and disfigured, as the life of man is not, to his imagination. Each man sees over his own experience a certain stain of error, whilst that of other men looks fair and ideal. Let any man go back to those delicious relations which make the beauty of his life, which have given him sincerest instruction and nourishment, he will shrink and moan. Alas! I know not why, but infinite compunctions embitter in mature life the remembrances of budding joy, and cover every beloved name. Every thing is beautiful seen from the point of the intellect, or as truth. But all is sour, if seen as experience. Details are melancholy; the plan is seemly and noble. In the actual world—the painful kingdom of time and place—dwell care, and canker, and fear. With thought, with the ideal, is immortal hilarity, the rose of joy. Round it all the Muses sing. But grief cleaves to names, and persons, and the partial interests of to-day and yesterday.

The strong bent of nature is seen in the proportion which this topic of personal relations usurps in the

conversation of society. What do we wish to know of any worthy person so much, as how he has sped in the history of this sentiment? What books in the circulating libraries circulate? How we glow over these novels of passion, when the story is told with any spark of truth and nature! And what fastens attention, in the intercourse of life, like any passage betraying affection between two parties? Perhaps we never saw them before, and never shall meet them again. But we see them exchange a glance, or betray a deep emotion, and we are no longer strangers. We understand them, and take the warmest interest in the development of the romance. All mankind love a lover. The earliest demonstrations of complacency and kindness are nature's most winning pictures. It is the dawn of civility and grace in the coarse and rustic. The rude village boy teases the girls about the school-house door;—but to-day he comes running into the entry, and meets one fair child disposing her satchel; he holds her books to help her, and instantly it seems to him as if she removed herself from him infinitely, and was a sacred precinct. Among the throng of girls he runs rudely enough, but one alone distances him; and these two little neighbours, that were so close just now, have learned to respect each other's personality. Or who can avert his eyes from the engaging, half-artful, half-artless ways of school-girls who go into the country shops to buy a skein of silk or a sheet of paper, and talk

half an hour about nothing with the broad-faced, good-natured shop-boy. In the village they are on a perfect equality, which love delights in, and without any coquetry the happy, affectionate nature of woman flows out in this pretty gossip. The girls may have little beauty, yet plainly do they establish between them and the good boy the most agreeable, confiding relations, what with their fun and their earnest, about Edgar, and Jonas, and Almira, and who was invited to the party, and who danced at the dancing-school, and when the singing-school would begin, and other nothings concerning which the parties cooed. By and by that boy wants a wife, and very truly and heartily will he know where to find a sincere and sweet mate, without any risk such as Milton deplores as incident to scholars and great men.

I have been told, that in some public discourses of mine my reverence for the intellect has made me unjustly cold to the personal relations. But now I almost shrink at the remembrance of such disparaging words. For persons are love's world, and the coldest philosopher cannot recount the debt of the young soul wandering here in nature to the power of love, without being tempted to unsay, as treasonable to nature, aught derogatory to the social instincts. For, though the celestial rapture falling out of heaven seizes only upon those of tender age, and although a beauty overpowering all analysis or comparison, and putting us quite beside ourselves, we can seldom see after thirty years, yet the remembrance of these visions outlasts all other remembrances, and is a wreath of flowers on the oldest brows. But here is a strange fact; it may seem to many men, in revising their experience, that they have no fairer page in their life's book than the delicious memory of some passages wherein affection contrived to give a witchcraft surpassing the deep attraction of its own truth to a parcel of accidental and trivial circumstances. In looking backward, they may find that several things which were not the charm have more reality to this groping memory than the charm itself which embalmed them. But be our experience in particulars what it may, no man ever forgot the visitations of that power to his heart and brain, which created all things new; which was the dawn in him of music, poetry, and art; which made the face of nature radiant with purple light, the morning and the night varied enchantments; when a single tone of one voice could make the heart bound, and the most trivial circumstance associated with one form is put in the amber of memory; when he became all eye when one was present, and all memory when one was gone; when the youth becomes a watcher of windows, and studious of a glove, a veil, a ribbon, or the wheels of a carriage; when no place is too solitary, and none too silent, for him who has richer company and sweeter conversation in his new thoughts, than any

old friends, though best and purest, can give him; for the figures, the motions, the words of the beloved object are not like other images written in water, but, as Plutarch said, "enamelled in fire," and make the study of midnight.

> "Thou art not gone being gone, where'er thou
>   art,
> Thou leav'st in him thy watchful eyes, in him thy
>   loving heart."

In the noon and the afternoon of life we still throb at the recollection of days when happiness was not happy enough, but must be drugged with the relish of pain and fear; for he touched the secret of the matter, who said of love, —

> "All other pleasures are not worth its pains";

and when the day was not long enough, but the night, too, must be consumed in keen recollections; when the head boiled all night on the pillow with the generous deed it resolved on; when the moonlight was a pleasing fever, and the stars were letters, and the flowers ciphers, and the air was coined into song; when all business seemed an impertinence, and all the men and women running to and fro in the streets, mere pictures.

The passion rebuilds the world for the youth. It makes all things alive and significant. Nature grows conscious. Every bird on the boughs of the tree sings now to his heart and soul. The notes are almost articulate. The clouds have faces as he looks on them. The trees of the forest, the waving grass, and the peeping flowers have grown intelligent; and he almost fears to trust them with the secret which they seem to invite. Yet nature soothes and sympathizes. In the green solitude he finds a dearer home than with men.

> "Fountain-heads and pathless groves,
> Places which pale passion loves,
> Moonlight walks, when all the fowls
> Are safely housed, save bats and owls,
> A midnight bell, a passing groan, —
> These are the sounds we feed upon."

Behold there in the wood the fine madman! He is a palace of sweet sounds and sights; he dilates; he is twice a man; he walks with arms akimbo; he soliloquizes; he accosts the grass and the trees; he feels the blood of the violet, the clover, and the lily in his veins; and he talks with the brook that wets his foot.

The heats that have opened his perceptions of natural beauty have made him love music and verse. It is a fact often observed, that men have written good verses under

the inspiration of passion, who cannot write well under any other circumstances.

The like force has the passion over all his nature. It expands the sentiment; it makes the clown gentle, and gives the coward heart. Into the most pitiful and abject it will infuse a heart and courage to defy the world, so only it have the countenance of the beloved object. In giving him to another, it still more gives him to himself. He is a new man, with new perceptions, new and keener purposes, and a religious solemnity of character and aims. He does not longer appertain to his family and society; *he* is somewhat; *he* is a person; *he* is a soul.

And here let us examine a little nearer the nature of that influence which is thus potent over the human youth. Beauty, whose revelation to man we now celebrate, welcome as the sun wherever it pleases to shine, which pleases everybody with it and with themselves, seems sufficient to itself. The lover cannot paint his maiden to his fancy poor and solitary. Like a tree in flower, so much soft, budding, informing love-liness is society for itself, and she teaches his eye why Beauty was pictured with Loves and Graces attending her steps. Her existence makes the world rich. Though she extrudes all other persons from his attention as cheap and unworthy, she indemnifies him by carrying out her own being into somewhat impersonal, large, mundane, so that the maiden stands to him for a repre-

sentative of all select things and virtues. For that reason, the lover never sees personal resemblances in his mistress to her kindred or to others. His friends find in her a likeness to her mother, or her sisters, or to persons not of her blood. The lover sees no resemblance except to summer evenings and diamond mornings, to rainbows and the song of birds.

The ancients called beauty the flowering of virtue. Who can analyze the nameless charm which glances from one and another face and form? We are touched with emotions of tenderness and complacency, but we cannot find whereat this dainty emotion, this wandering gleam, points. It is destroyed for the imagination by any attempt to refer it to organization. Nor does it point to any relations of friendship or love known and described in society, but, as it seems to me, to a quite other and unattainable sphere, to relations of transcendent delicacy and sweetness, to what roses and violets hint and fore-show. We cannot approach beauty. Its nature is like opaline doves'-neck lustres, hovering and evanescent. Herein it resembles the most excellent things, which all have this rainbow character, defying all attempts at appropriation and use. What else did Jean Paul Richter signify, when he said to music, "Away! away! thou speakest to me of things which in all my endless life I have not found, and shall not find." The same fluency may be observed in every work of the

plastic arts. The statue is then beautiful when it begins to be incomprehensible, when it is passing out of criticism, and can no longer be defined by compass and measuring-wand, but demands an active imagination to go with it, and to say what it is in the act of doing. The god or hero of the sculptor is always represented in a transition *from* that which is representable to the senses, *to* that which is not. Then first it ceases to be a stone. The same remark holds of painting. And of poetry, the success is not attained when it lulls and satisfies, but when it astonishes and fires us with new endeavors after the unattainable. Concerning it, Landor inquires "whether it is not to be referred to some purer state of sensation and existence."

In like manner, personal beauty is then first charming and itself, when it dissatisfies us with any end; when it becomes a story without an end; when it suggests gleams and visions, and not earthly satisfactions; when it makes the beholder feel his unworthiness; when he cannot feel his right to it, though he were Caesar; he cannot feel more right to it than to the firmament and the splendors of a sunset.

Hence arose the saying, "If I love you, what is that to you?" We say so, because we feel that what we love is not in your will, but above it. It is not you, but your radiance. It is that which you know not in yourself, and can never know.

This agrees well with that high philosophy of Beauty which the ancient writers delighted in; for they said that the soul of man, embodied here on earth, went roaming up and down in quest of that other world of its own, out of which it came into this, but was soon stupefied by the light of the natural sun, and unable to see any other objects than those of this world, which are but shadows of real things. Therefore, the Deity sends the glory of youth before the soul, that it may avail itself of beautiful bodies as aids to its recollection of the celestial good and fair; and the man beholding such a person in the female sex runs to her, and finds the highest joy in contemplating the form, movement, and intelligence of this person, because it suggests to him the presence of that which indeed is within the beauty, and the cause of the beauty.

If, however, from too much conversing with material objects, the soul was gross, and misplaced its satisfaction in the body, it reaped nothing but sorrow; body being unable to fulfil the promise which beauty holds out; but if, accepting the hint of these visions and suggestions which beauty makes to his mind, the soul passes through the body, and falls to admire strokes of character, and the lovers contemplate one another in their discourses and their actions, then they pass to the true palace of beauty, more and more inflame their love of it, and by this love extinguishing the base affection, as the sun

puts out the fire by shining on the hearth, they become pure and hallowed. By conversation with that which is in itself excellent, magnanimous, lowly, and just, the lover comes to a warmer love of these nobilities, and a quicker apprehension of them. Then he passes from loving them in one to loving them in all, and so is the one beautiful soul only the door through which he enters to the society of all true and pure souls. In the particular society of his mate, he attains a clearer sight of any spot, any taint, which her beauty has contracted from this world, and is able to point it out, and this with mutual joy that they are now able, without offence, to indicate blemishes and hindrances in each other, and give to each all help and comfort in curing the same. And, beholding in many souls the traits of the divine beauty, and separating in each soul that which is divine from the taint which it has contracted in the world, the lover ascends to the highest beauty, to the love and knowledge of the Divinity, by steps on this ladder of created souls.

Somewhat like this have the truly wise told us of love in all ages. The doctrine is not old, nor is it new. If Plato, Plutarch, and Apuleius taught it, so have Petrarch, Angelo, and Milton. It awaits a truer unfolding in opposition and rebuke to that subterranean prudence which presides at marriages with words that take hold of the upper world, whilst one eye is prowling in the cellar, so that its gravest discourse has a savor of hams and powdering-tubs. Worst, when this sensualism intrudes into the education of young women, and withers the hope and affection of human nature, by teaching that marriage signifies nothing but a house-wife's thrift, and that woman's life has no other aim.

But this dream of love, though beautiful, is only one scene in our play. In the procession of the soul from within outward, it enlarges its circles ever, like the pebble thrown into the pond, or the light proceeding from an orb. The rays of the soul alight first on things nearest, on every utensil and toy, on nurses and domestics, on the house, and yard, and passengers, on the circle of household acquaintance, on politics, and geography, and history. But things are ever grouping themselves according to higher or more interior laws. Neighbor-hood, size, numbers, habits, persons, lose by degrees their power over us. Cause and effect, real affinities, the longing for harmony between the soul and the circum-stance, the progressive, idealizing instinct, predominate later, and the step backward from the higher to the lower relations is impossible. Thus even love, which is the deification of persons, must become more impersonal every day. Of this at first it gives no hint. Little think the youth and maiden who are glancing at each other across crowded rooms, with eyes so full of mutual intel-ligence, of the precious fruit long hereafter to proceed from this new, quite external stimulus. The work of

vegetation begins first in the irritability of the bark and leaf-buds. From exchanging glances, they advance to acts of courtesy, of gallantry, then to fiery passion, to plighting troth, and marriage. Passion beholds its object as a perfect unit. The soul is wholly embodied, and the body is wholly ensouled.

"Her pure and eloquent blood
Spoke in her cheeks, and so distinctly wrought,
That one might almost say her body thought."

Romeo, if dead, should be cut up into little stars to make the heavens fine. Life, with this pair, has no other aim, asks no more, than Juliet,—than Romeo. Night, day, studies, talents, kingdoms, religion, are all contained in this form full of soul, in this soul which is all form. The lovers delight in endearments, in avowals of love, in comparisons of their regards. When alone, they solace themselves with the remembered image of the other. Does that other see the same star, the same melting cloud, read the same book, feel the same emotion, that now delight me? They try and weigh their affection, and, adding up costly advantages, friends, opportunities, properties, exult in discovering that willingly, joyfully, they would give all as a ransom for the beautiful, the beloved head, not one hair of which shall be harmed. But the lot of humanity is on

these children. Danger, sorrow, and pain arrive to them, as to all. Love prays. It makes covenants with Eternal Power in behalf of this dear mate. The union which is thus effected, and which adds a new value to every atom in nature, for it transmutes every thread throughout the whole web of relation into a golden ray, and bathes the soul in a new and sweeter element, is yet a temporary state. Not always can flowers, pearls, poetry, protestations, nor even home in another heart, content the awful soul that dwells in clay. It arouses itself at last from these endearments, as toys, and puts on the harness, and aspires to vast and universal aims. The soul which is in the soul of each, craving a perfect beatitude, detects incongruities, defects, and disproportion in the behaviour of the other. Hence arise surprise, expostulation, and pain. Yet that which drew them to each other was signs of loveliness, signs of virtue; and these virtues are there, however eclipsed. They appear and reappear, and continue to attract; but the regard changes, quits the sign, and attaches to the substance. This repairs the wounded affection. Meantime, as life wears on, it proves a game of permutation and combination of all possible positions of the parties, to employ all the resources of each, and acquaint each with the strength and weakness of the other. For it is the nature and end of this relation, that they should represent the human race to each other. All that is in the world, which

is or ought to be known, is cunningly wrought into the texture of man, of woman.

"The person love does to us fit,
Like manna, has the taste of all in it."

The world rolls; the circumstances vary every hour. The angels that inhabit this temple of the body appear at the windows, and the gnomes and vices also. By all the virtues they are united. If there be virtue, all the vices are known as such; they confess and flee. Their once flaming regard is sobered by time in either breast, and, losing in violence what it gains in extent, it becomes a thorough good understanding. They resign each other, without complaint, to the good offices which man and woman are severally appointed to discharge in time, and exchange the passion which once could not lose sight of its object, for a cheerful, disengaged furtherance, whether present or absent, of each other's designs. At last they discover that all which at first drew them together,— those once sacred features, that magical play of charms,—was deciduous, had a prospective end, like the scaffolding by which the house was built; and the purification of the intellect and the heart, from year to year, is the real marriage, foreseen and prepared from the first, and wholly above their consciousness. Looking at these aims with which two persons, a man and a woman, so variously

and correlatively gifted, are shut up in one house to spend in the nuptial society forty or fifty years, I do not wonder at the emphasis with which the heart prophesies this crisis from early infancy, at the profuse beauty with which the instincts deck the nuptial bower, and nature, and intellect, and art emulate each other in the gifts and the melody they bring to the epithalamium.

Thus are we put in training for a love which knows not sex, nor person, nor partiality, but which seeks virtue and wisdom everywhere, to the end of increasing virtue and wisdom. We are by nature observers, and thereby learners. That is our permanent state. But we are often made to feel that our affections are but tents of a night. Though slowly and with pain, the objects of the affections change, as the objects of thought do. There are moments when the affections rule and absorb the man, and make his happiness dependent on a person or persons. But in health the mind is presently seen again,—its overarching vault, bright with galaxies of immutable lights, and the warm loves and fears that swept over us as clouds, must lose their finite character and blend with God, to attain their own perfection. But we need not fear that we can lose any thing by the progress of the soul. The soul may be trusted to the end. That which is so beautiful and attractive as these relations must be succeeded and supplanted only by what is more beautiful, and so on for ever.

Prudence

Theme no poet gladly sung,
Fair to old and foul to young,
Scorn not thou the love of parts,
And the articles of arts.
Grandeur of the perfect sphere
Thanks the atoms that cohere.

What right have I to write ont of the negative sort? My prudence consists in avoiding and going without, not in the inventing of means and methods, not in adroit steering, not in gentle repairing. I have no skill to make money spend well, no genius in my economy, and whoever sees my garden discovers that I must have some other garden. Yet I love facts, and hate lubricity, and people without perception. Then I have the same title to write on prudence, that I have to write on poetry or holiness. We write from aspiration and antagonism, as well as from experience. We paint those qualities which we do not possess. The poet

admires the man of energy and tactics; the merchant breeds his son for the church or the bar: and where a man is not vain and egotistic, you shall find what he has not by his praise. Moreover, it would be hardly honest in me not to balance these fine lyric words of Love and Friendship with words of coarser sound, and, whilst my debt to my senses is real and constant, not to own it in passing.

Prudence is the virtue of the senses. It is the science of appearances. It is the outmost action of the inward life. It is God taking thought for oxen. It moves matter after the laws of matter. It is content to seek health of body by complying with physical conditions, and health of mind by the laws of the intellect.

The world of the senses is a world of shows; it does not exist for itself, but has a symbolic character; and a true prudence or law of shows recognizes the copresence of other laws, and knows that its own office is subaltern; knows that it is surface and not centre where it works. Prudence is false when detached. It is legitimate when it is the Natural History of the soul incarnate; when it unfolds the beauty of laws within the narrow scope of the senses.

There are all degrees of proficiency in knowledge of the world. It is sufficient, to our present purpose, to indicate three. One class live to the utility of the symbol; esteeming health and wealth a final good. Another class

live above this mark to the beauty of the symbol; as the poet, and artist, and the naturalist, and man of science. A third class live above the beauty of the symbol to the beauty of the thing signified; these are wise men. The first class have common sense; the second, taste; and the third, spiritual perception. Once in a long time, a man traverses the whole scale, and sees and enjoys the symbol solidly; then also has a clear eye for its beauty, and, lastly, whilst he pitches his tent on this sacred volcanic isle of nature, does not offer to build houses and barns thereon, reverencing the splendor of the God which he sees bursting through each chink and cranny.

The world is filled with the proverbs and acts and winkings of a base prudence, which is a devotion to matter, as if we possessed no other faculties than the palate, the nose, the touch, the eye and ear; a prudence which adores the Rule of Three, which never subscribes, which never gives, which seldom lends, and asks but one question of any project,—Will it bake bread? This is a disease like a thickening of the skin until the vital organs are destroyed. But culture, revealing the high origin of the apparent world, and aiming at the perfection of the man as the end, degrades every thing else, as health and bodily life, into means. It sees prudence not to be a several faculty, but a name for wisdom and virtue conversing with the body and its wants. Cultivated men always feel and speak so, as if a

great fortune, the achievement of a civil or social measure, great personal influence, a graceful and commanding address, had their value as proofs of the energy of the spirit. If a man lose his balance, and immerse himself in any trades or pleasures for their own sake, he may be a good wheel or pin, but he is not a cultivated man.

The spurious prudence, making the senses final, is the god of sots and cowards, and is the subject of all comedy. It is nature's joke, and therefore literature's. The true prudence limits this sensualism by admitting the knowledge of an internal and real world. This recognition once made,—the order of the world and the distribution of affairs and times being studied with the co-perception of their subordinate place, will reward any degree of attention. For our existence, thus apparently attached in nature to the sun and the returning moon and the periods which they mark,—so susceptible to climate and to country, so alive to social good and evil, so fond of splendor, and so tender to hunger and cold and debt,—reads all its primary lessons out of these books.

Prudence does not go behind nature, and ask whence it is. It takes the laws of the world, whereby man's being is conditioned, as they are, and keeps these laws that it may enjoy their proper good. It respects space and time, climate, want, sleep, the law of polarity, growth and

death. There revolve, to give bound and period to his being, on all sides, the sun and moon, the great formalists in the sky: here lies stubborn matter, and will not swerve from its chemical routine. Here is a planted globe, pierced and belted with natural laws, and fenced and distributed externally with civil partitions and properties which impose new restraints on the young inhabitant.

We eat of the bread which grows in the field. We live by the air which blows around us, and we are poisoned by the air that is too cold or too hot, too dry or too wet. Time, which shows so vacant, indivisible, and divine in its coming, is slit and peddled into trifles and tatters. A door is to be painted, a lock to be repaired. I want wood, or oil, or meal, or salt; the house smokes, or I have a headache; then the tax; and an affair to be transacted with a man without heart or brains; and the stinging recollection of an injurious or very awkward word,—these eat up the hours. Do what we can, summer will have its flies: if we walk in the woods, we must feed mosquitos: if we go a-fishing, we must expect a wet coat. Then climate is a great impediment to idle persons: we often resolve to give up the care of the weather, but still we regard the clouds and the rain.

We are instructed by these petty experiences which usurp the hours and years. The hard soil and four months of snow make the inhabitant of the northern temperate zone wiser and abler than his fellow who enjoys the fixed smile of the tropics. The islander may ramble all day at will. At night, he may sleep on a mat under the moon, and wherever a wild date-tree grows, nature has, without a prayer even, spread a table for his morning meal. The northerner is perforce a house-holder. He must brew, bake, salt, and preserve his food, and pile wood and coal. But as it happens that not one stroke can labor lay to, without some new acquaintance with nature; and as nature is inexhaustibly significant, the inhabitants of these climates have always excelled the southerner in force. Such is the value of these matters, that a man who knows other things can never know too much of these. Let him have accurate percep-tions. Let him, if he have hands, handle; if eyes, measure and discriminate; let him accept and hive every fact of chemistry, natural history, and economics; the more he has, the less is he willing to spare any one. Time is always bringing the occasions that disclose their value. Some wisdom comes out of every natural and innocent action. The domestic man, who loves no music so well as his kitchen clock, and the airs which the logs sing to him as they burn on the hearth, has solaces which others never dream of. The application of means to ends insures victory and the songs of victory, not less in a farm or a shop than in the tactics of party or of war. The good husband finds method as efficient in the packing of

fire-wood in a shed, or in the harvesting of fruits in the cellar, as in Peninsular campaigns or the files of the Department of State. In the rainy day, he builds a work-bench, or gets his tool-box set in the corner of the barn-chamber, and stored with nails, gimlet, pincers, screwdriver, and chisel. Herein he tastes an old joy of youth and childhood, the cat-like love of garrets, presses, and corn-chambers, and of the conveniences of long housekeeping. His garden or his poultry-yard tells him many pleasant anecdotes. One might find argument for optimism in the abundant flow of this saccharine element of pleasure in every suburb and extremity of the good world. Let a man keep the law,—any law,—and his way will be strown with satisfactions. There is more difference in the quality of our pleasures than in the amount.

On the other hand, nature punishes any neglect of prudence. If you think the senses final, obey their law. If you believe in the soul, do not clutch at sensual sweetness before it is ripe on the slow tree of cause and effect. It is vinegar to the eyes, to deal with men of loose and imperfect perception. Dr. Johnson is reported to have said,—"If the child says he looked out of this window, when he looked out of that,—whip him." Our American character is marked by a more than average delight in accurate perception, which is shown by the currency of the byword, "No mistake." But the

discomfort of unpunctuality, of confusion of thought about facts, of inattention to the wants of to-morrow, is of no nation. The beautiful laws of time and space, once dislocated by our inaptitude, are holes and dens. If the hive be disturbed by rash and stupid hands, instead of honey, it will yield us bees. Our words and actions to be fair must be timely. A gay and pleasant sound is the whetting of the scythe in the mornings of June; yet what is more lonesome and sad than the sound of a whetstone or mower's rifle, when it is too late in the season to make hay? Scatter-brained and "afternoon men" spoil much more than their own affair, in spoiling the temper of those who deal with them. I have seen a criticism on some paintings, of which I am reminded when I see the shiftless and unhappy men who are not true to their senses. The last Grand Duke of Weimar, a man of superior understanding, said:—"I have sometimes remarked in the presence of great works of art, and just now especially, in Dresden, how much a certain property contributes to the effect which gives life to the figures, and to the life an irresistible truth. This property is the hitting, in all the figures we draw, the right centre of gravity. I mean, the placing the figures firm upon their feet, making the hands grasp, and fastening the eyes on the spot where they should look. Even lifeless figures, as vessels and stools,—let them be drawn ever so correctly,—lose all effect so soon as they

lack the resting upon their centre of gravity, and have a certain swimming and oscillating appearance. The Raphael, in the Dresden gallery, (the only greatly affecting picture which I have seen,) is the quietest and most passionless piece you can imagine; a couple of saints who worship the Virgin and Child. Nevertheless, it awakens a deeper impression than the contortions of ten crucified martyrs. For, beside all the resistless beauty of form, it possesses in the highest degree the property of the perpendicularity of all the figures." This perpendicularity we demand of all the figures in this picture of life. Let them stand on their feet, and not float and swing. Let us know where to find them. Let them discriminate between what they remember and what they dreamed, call a spade a spade, give us facts, and honor their own senses with trust.

But what man shall dare tax another with imprudence? Who is prudent? The men we call greatest are least in this kingdom. There is a certain fatal dislocation in our relation to nature, distorting our modes of living, and making every law our enemy, which seems at last to have aroused all the wit and virtue in the world to ponder the question of Reform. We must call the highest prudence to counsel, and ask why health and beauty and genius should now be the exception, rather than the rule, of human nature? We do not know the properties of plants and animals and the laws of nature through our sympathy with the same; but this remains the dream of poets. Poetry and prudence should be coincident. Poets should be lawgivers; that is, the boldest lyric inspiration should not chide and insult, but should announce and lead, the civil code, and the day's work. But now the two things seem irreconcilably parted. We have violated law upon law, until we stand amidst ruins, and when by chance we espy a coincidence between reason and the phenomena, we are surprised. Beauty should be the dowry of every man and woman, as invariably as sensation; but it is rare. Health or sound organization should be universal. Genius should be the child of genius, and every child should be inspired; but now it is not to be predicted of any child, and nowhere is it pure. We call partial half-lights, by courtesy, genius; talent which converts itself to money; talent which glitters to-day, that it may dine and sleep well to-morrow; and society is officered by *men of parts*, as they are properly called, and not by divine men. These use their gifts to refine luxury, not to abolish it. Genius is always ascetic; and piety and love. Appetite shows to the finer souls as a disease, and they find beauty in rites and bounds that resist it.

We have found out fine names to cover our sensuality withal, but no gifts can raise intemperance. The man of talent affects to call his transgressions of the laws of the senses trivial, and to count them nothing considered

with his devotion to his art. His art never taught him lewdness, nor the love of wine, nor the wish to reap where he had not sowed. His art is less for every deduction from his holiness, and less for every defect of common sense. On him who scorned the world, as he said, the scorned world wreaks its revenge. He that despiseth small things will perish by little and little. Goethe's Tasso is very likely to be a pretty fair historical portrait, and that is true tragedy. It does not seem to me so genuine grief when some tyrannous Richard the Third oppresses and slays a score of innocent persons, as when Antonio and Tasso, both apparently right, wrong each other. One living after the maxims of this world, and consistent and true to them, the other fired with all divine sentiments, yet grasping also at the pleasures of sense, without submitting to their law. That is a grief we all feel, a knot we cannot untie. Tasso's is no infrequent case in modern biography. A man of genius, of an ardent temperament, reckless of physical laws, self-indulgent, becomes presently unfortunate, querulous, a "discomfortable cousin," a thorn to himself and to others.

The scholar shames us by his bifold life. Whilst something higher than prudence is active, he is admirable; when common sense is wanted, he is an encumbrance. Yesterday, Caesar was not so great; to-day, the felon at the gallows' foot is not more miserable.

Yesterday, radiant with the light of an ideal world, in which he lives, the first of men; and now oppressed by wants and by sickness, for which he must thank himself. He resembles the pitiful drivellers, whom travellers describe as frequenting the bazaars of Constantinople, who skulk about all day, yellow, emaciated, ragged, sneaking; and at evening, when the bazaars are open, slink to the opium-shop, swallow their morsel, and become tranquil and glorified seers. And who has not seen the tragedy of imprudent genius, struggling for years with paltry pecuniary difficulties, at last sinking, chilled, exhausted, and fruitless, like a giant slaughtered by pins?

Is it not better that a man should accept the first pains and mortifications of this sort, which nature is not slack in sending him, as hints that he must expect no other good than the just fruit of his own labor and self-denial? Health, bread, climate, social position, have their importance, and he will give them their due. Let him esteem Nature a perpetual counsellor, and her perfections the exact measure of our deviations. Let him make the night night, and the day day. Let him control the habit of expense. Let him see that as much wisdom may be expended on a private economy as on an empire, and as much wisdom may be drawn from it. The laws of the world are written out for him on every piece of money in his hand. There is nothing he will not be the

better for knowing, were it only the wisdom of Poor Richard; or the State-Street prudence of buying by the acre to sell by the foot; or the thrift of the agriculturist, to stick a tree between whiles, because it will grow whilst he sleeps; or the prudence which consists in husbanding little strokes of the tool, little portions of time, particles of stock, and small gains. The eye of prudence may never shut. Iron, if kept at the ironmonger's, will rust; beer, if not brewed in the right state of the atmosphere, will sour; timber of ships will rot at sea, or, if laid up high and dry, will strain, warp, and dry-rot; money, if kept by us, yields no rent, and is liable to loss; if invested, is liable to depreciation of the particular kind of stock. Strike, says the smith, the iron is white; keep the rake, says the haymaker, as nigh the scythe as you can, and the cart as nigh the rake. Our Yankee trade is reputed to be very much on the extreme of this prudence. It takes bank-notes,—good, bad, clean, ragged,—and saves itself by the speed with which it passes them off. Iron cannot rust, nor beer sour, nor timber rot, nor calicoes go out of fashion, nor money stocks depreciate, in the few swift moments in which the Yankee suffers any one of them to remain in his possession. In skating over thin ice, our safety is in our speed.

Let him learn a prudence of a higher strain. Let him learn that every thing in nature, even motes and feathers, go by law and not by luck, and that what he sows he

reaps. By diligence and self-command, let him put the bread he eats at his own disposal, that he may not stand in bitter and false relations to other men; for the best good of wealth is freedom. Let him practise the minor virtues. How much of human life is lost in waiting! let him not make his fellow-creatures wait. How many words and promises are promises of conversation! let his be words of fate. When he sees a folded and sealed scrap of paper float round the globe in a pine ship, and come safe to the eye for which it was written, amidst a swarming population, let him likewise feel the admonition to integrate his being across all these distracting forces, and keep a slender human word among the storms, distances, and accidents that drive us hither and thither, and, by persistency, make the paltry force of one man reappear to redeem its pledge, after months and years, in the most distant climates.

We must not try to write the laws of any one virtue, looking at that only. Human nature loves no contradictions, but is symmetrical. The prudence which secures an outward well-being is not to be studied by one set of men, whilst heroism and holiness are studied by another, but they are reconcilable. Prudence concerns the present time, persons, property, and existing forms. But as every fact hath its roots in the soul, and, if the soul were changed, would cease to be, or would become some other thing, the proper administration of outward

things will always rest on a just apprehension of their cause and origin, that is, the good man will be the wise man, and the single-hearted, the politic man. Every violation of truth is not only a sort of suicide in the liar, but is a stab at the health of human society. On the most profitable lie, the course of events presently lays a destructive tax; whilst frankness invites frankness, puts the parties on a convenient footing, and makes their business a friendship. Trust men, and they will be true to you; treat them greatly, and they will show themselves great, though they make an exception in your favor to all their rules of trade.

So, in regard to disagreeable and formidable things, prudence does not consist in evasion, or in flight, but in courage. He who wishes to walk in the most peaceful parts of life with any serenity must screw himself up to resolution. Let him front the object of his worst apprehension, and his stoutness will commonly make his fear groundless. The Latin proverb says, that "in battles the eye is first overcome." Entire self-possession may make a battle very little more dangerous to life than a match at foils or at football. Examples are cited by soldiers, of men who have seen the cannon pointed, and the fire given to it, and who have stepped aside from the path of the ball. The terrors of the storm are chiefly confined to the parlour and the cabin. The drover, the sailor, buffets it all day, and his health renews itself at as vigorous

a pulse under the sleet, as under the sun of June.

In the occurrence of unpleasant things among neighbours, fear comes readily to heart, and magnifies the consequence of the other party; but it is a bad counsellor. Every man is actually weak, and apparently strong.

To himself, he seems weak; to others, formidable. You are afraid of Grim; but Grim also is afraid of you. You are solicitous of the good-will of the meanest person, uneasy at his ill-will. But the sturdiest offender of your peace and of the neighborhood, if you rip up *his* claims, is as thin and timid as any; and the peace of society is often kept, because, as children say, one is afraid, and the other dares not. Far off, men swell, bully, and threaten; bring them hand to hand, and they are a feeble folk.

It is a proverb, that 'courtesy costs nothing'; but calculation might come to value love for its profit. Love is fabled to be blind; but kindness is necessary to perception; love is not a hood, but an eye-water. If you meet a sectary, or a hostile partisan, never recognize the dividing lines; but meet on what common ground remains,—if only that the sun shines, and the rain rains for both; the area will widen very fast, and ere you know it the boundary mountains, on which the eye had fastened, have melted into air. If they set out to contend, Saint Paul will lie, and Saint John will hate. What low, poor, paltry, hypocritical people an argument on religion

will make of the pure and chosen souls! They will shuffle, and crow, crook, and hide, feign to confess here, only that they may brag and conquer there, and not a thought has enriched either party, and not an emotion of bravery, modesty, or hope. So neither should you put yourself in a false position with your contemporaries, by indulging a vein of hostility and bitterness. Though your views are in straight antagonism to theirs, assume an identity of sentiment, assume that you are saying precisely that which all think, and in the flow of wit and love roll out your paradoxes in solid column, with not the infirmity of a doubt. So at least shall you get an adequate deliverance. The natural motions of the soul are so much better than the voluntary ones, that you will never do yourself justice in dispute. The thought is not then taken hold of by the right handle, does not show itself proportioned, and in its true bearings, but bears extorted, hoarse, and half witness. But assume a consent, and it shall presently be granted, since, really, and underneath their external diversities, all men are of one heart and mind.

Wisdom will never let us stand with any man or men on an unfriendly footing. We refuse sympathy and intimacy with people, as if we waited for some better sympathy and intimacy to come. But whence and when? To-morrow will be like to-day. Life wastes itself whilst we are preparing to live. Our friends and fellow-workers die off from us. Scarcely can we say, we see new men, new women, approaching us. We are too old to regard fashion, too old to expect patronage of any greater or more powerful. Let us suck the sweetness of those affections and consuetudes that grow near us. These old shoes are easy to the feet. Undoubtedly, we can easily pick faults in our company, can easily whisper names prouder, and that tickle the fancy more. Every man's imagination hath its friends; and life would be dearer with such companions. But, if you cannot have them on good mutual terms, you cannot have them. If not the Deity, but our ambition, hews and shapes the new relations, their virtue escapes, as strawberries lose their flavor in garden-beds.

Thus truth, frankness, courage, love, humility, and all the virtues, range themselves on the side of prudence, or the art of securing a present well-being. I do not know if all matter will be found to be made of one element, as oxygen or hydrogen, at last, but the world of manners and actions is wrought of one stuff, and, begin where we will, we are pretty sure in a short space to be mumbling our ten commandments.

Heroism

"Paradise is under the shadow of swords."
Mahomet

Ruby wine is drunk by knaves,
Sugar spends to fatten slaves,
Rose and vine-leaf deck buffoons;
Thunderclouds are Jove's festoons,
Drooping oft in wreaths of dread
Lightning-knotted round his head;
The hero is not fed on sweets,
Daily his own heart he eats;
Chambers of the great are jails,
And head-winds right for royal sails.

In the elder English dramaetcher, there is a constant
recognition of gentility, as if a noble behavior were as
easily marked in the society of their age, as color is in
our American population. When any Rodrigo, Pedro, or

Valerio enters, though he be a stranger, the duke or governor exclaims, This is a gentleman,—and proffers civilities without end; but all the rest are slag and refuse. In harmony with this delight in personal advantages, there is in their plays a certain heroic cast of character and dialogue,—as in Bonduca, Sophocles, the Mad Lover, the Double Marriage,—wherein the speaker is so earnest and cordial, and on such deep grounds of character, that the dialogue, on the slightest additional incident in the plot, rises naturally into poetry. Among many texts, take the following. The Roman Martius has conquered Athens,— all but the invincible spirits of Sophocles, the duke of Athens, and Dorigen, his wife. The beauty of the latter inflames Martius, and he seeks to save her husband; but Sophocles will not ask his life, although assured that a word will save him, and the execution of both proceeds.

"*Valerius.* Bid thy wife farewell.

Soph. No, I will take no leave. My Dorigen,
Yonder, above, 'bout Ariadne's crown,
My spirit shall hover for thee. Prithee, haste.

Dor. Stay, Sophocles,—with this tie up my sight;
Let not soft nature so transformed be,
And lose her gentler sexed humanity,
To make me see my lord bleed. So, 't is well;

Never one object underneath the sun
Will I behold before my Sophocles:
Farewell; now teach the Romans how to die.

Mar. Dost know what 't is to die?

Soph. Thou dost not, Martius,
And, therefore, not what 't is to live; to die
Is to begin to live. It is to end
An old, stale, weary work, and to commence
A newer and a better. 'T is to leave
Deceitful knaves for the society
Of gods and goodness. Thou thyself must part
At last from all thy garlands, pleasures, triumphs,
And prove thy fortitude what then 't will do.

Val. But art not grieved nor vexed to leave thy
life thus?

Soph. Why should I grieve or vex for being sent
To them I ever loved best? Now I'll kneel,
But with my back toward thee; 't is the last duty
This trunk can do the gods.

Mar. Strike, strike, Valerius,
Or Martius' heart will leap out at his mouth:
This is a man, a woman! Kiss thy lord,

And live with all the freedom you were wont.
O love! thou doubly hast afflicted me
With virtue and with beauty. Treacherous heart,
My hand shall cast thee quick into my urn,
Ere thou transgress this knot of piety.

Val. What ails my brother?

Soph. Martius, O Martius,
Thou now hast found a way to conquer me.

Dor. O star of Rome! what gratitude can speak
Fit words to follow such a deed as this?

Mar. This admirable duke, Valerius,
With his disdain of fortune and of death,
Captived himself, has captivated me,

And though my arm hath ta'en his body here,
His soul hath subjugated Martius' soul.
By Romulus, he is all soul, I think;
He hath no flesh, and spirit cannot be gyved;
Then we have vanquished nothing; he is free,
And Martius walks now in captivity."

I do not readily remember any poem, play, sermon,
novel, or oration, that our press vents in the last few

years, which goes to the same tune. We have a great many flutes and flageolets, but not often the sound of any fife. Yet, Wordsworth's Laodamia, and the ode of "Dion," and some sonnets, have a certain noble music; and Scott will sometimes draw a stroke like the portrait of Lord Evandale, given by Balfour of Burley. Thomas Carlyle, with his natural taste for what is manly and daring in character, has suffered no heroic trait in his favorites to drop from his biographical and historical pictures. Earlier, Robert Burns has given us a song or two. In the *Harleian Miscellanies*, there is an account of the battle of Lutzen, which deserves to be read. And Simon Ockley's *History of the Saracens* recounts the prodigies of individual valor with admiration, all the more evident on the part of the narrator, that he seems to think that his place in Christian Oxford requires of him some proper protestations of abhorrence. But, if we explore the literature of Heroism, we shall quickly come to Plutarch, who is its Doctor and historian. To him we owe the Brasidas, the Dion, the Epaminondas, the Scipio of old, and I must think we are more deeply indebted to him than to all the ancient writers. Each of his *Lives* is a refutation to the despondency and cowardice of our religious and political theorists. A wild courage, a Stoicism not of the schools, but of the blood, shines in every anecdote, and has given that book its immense fame.

We need books of this tart cathartic virtue, more than books of political science, or of private economy. Life is a festival only to the wise. Seen from the nook and chimney-side of prudence, it wears a ragged and dangerous front. The violations of the laws of nature by our predecessors and our contemporaries are punished in us also. The disease and deformity around us certify the infraction of natural, intellectual, and moral laws, and often violation on violation to breed such compound misery. A lock-jaw that bends a man's head back to his heels, hydrophobia, that makes him bark at his wife and babes, insanity, that makes him eat grass; war, plague, cholera, famine, indicate a certain ferocity in nature, which, as it had its inlet by human crime, must have its outlet by human suffering. Unhappily, no man exists who has not in his own person become, to some amount, a stockholder in the sin, and so made himself liable to a share in the expiation.

Our culture, therefore, must not omit the arming of the man. Let him hear in season, that he is born into the state of war, and that the commonwealth and his own well-being require that he should not go dancing in the weeds of peace, but warned, self-collected, and neither defying nor dreading the thunder, let him take both reputation and life in his hand, and, with perfect urbanity, dare the gibbet and the mob by the absolute truth of his speech, and the rectitude of his behavior.

Towards all this external evil, the man within the breast assumes a warlike attitude, and affirms his ability to cope single-handed with the infinite army of enemies. To this military attitude of the soul we give the name of Heroism. Its rudest form is the contempt for safety and ease, which makes the attractiveness of war. It is a self-trust which slights the restraints of prudence, in the plenitude of its energy and power to repair the harms it may suffer. The hero is a mind of such balance that no disturbances can shake his will, but pleasantly, and, as it were, merrily, he advances to his own music, alike in frightful alarms and in the tipsy mirth of universal dissoluteness. There is somewhat not philosophical in heroism; there is somewhat not holy in it; it seems not to know that other souls are of one texture with it; it has pride; it is the extreme of individual nature. Nevertheless, we must profoundly revere it. There is somewhat in great actions, which does not allow us to go behind them. Heroism feels and never reasons, and therefore is always right; and although a different breeding, different religion, and greater intellectual activity would have modified or even reversed the particular action, yet for the hero that thing he does is the highest deed, and is not open to the censure of philosophers or divines. It is the avowal of the unschooled man, that he finds a quality in him that is negligent of expense, of health, of life, of danger, of hatred, of

reproach, and knows that his will is higher and more excellent than all actual and all possible antagonists.

Heroism works in contradiction to the voice of mankind, and in contradiction, for a time, to the voice of the great and good. Heroism is an obedience to a secret impulse of an individual's character. Now to no other man can its wisdom appear as it does to him, for every man must be supposed to see a little farther on his own proper path than any one else. Therefore, just and wise men take umbrage at his act, until after some little time be past: then they see it to be in unison with their acts. All prudent men see that the action is clean contrary to a sensual prosperity; for every heroic act measures itself by its contempt of some external good. But it finds its own success at last, and then the prudent also extol.

Self-trust is the essence of heroism. It is the state of the soul at war, and its ultimate objects are the last defiance of falsehood and wrong, and the power to bear all that can be inflicted by evil agents. It speaks the truth, and it is just, generous, hospitable, temperate, scornful of petty calculations, and scornful of being scorned. It persists; it is of an undaunted boldness, and of a fortitude not to be wearied out. Its jest is the littleness of common life. That false prudence which dotes on health and wealth is the butt and merriment of heroism. Heroism, like Plotinus, is almost ashamed

of its body. What shall it say, then, to the sugar-plums and cats'-cradles, to the toilet, compliments, quarrels, cards, and custard, which rack the wit of all society. What joys has kind nature provided for us dear creatures! There seems to be no interval between greatness and meanness. When the spirit is not master of the world, then it is its dupe. Yet the little man takes the great hoax so innocently, works in it so headlong and believing, is born red, and dies gray, arranging his toilet, attending on his own health, laying traps for sweet food and strong wine, setting his heart on a horse or a rifle, made happy with a little gossip or a little praise, that the great soul cannot choose but laugh at such earnest nonsense. "Indeed, these humble considerations make me out of love with greatness. What a disgrace is it to me to take note how many pairs of silk stockings thou hast, namely, these and those that were the peach-colored ones; or to bear the inventory of thy shirts, as one for superfluity, and one other for use!"

Citizens, thinking after the laws of arithmetic, consider the inconvenience of receiving strangers at their fireside, reckon narrowly the loss of time and the unusual display: the soul of a better quality thrusts back the unseasonable economy into the vaults of life, and says, I will obey the God, and the sacrifice and the fire he will provide. Ibn Haukal, the Arabian geographer, describes a heroic extreme in the hospitality of Sogd, in Bukharia. "When I was in Sogd, I saw a great building, like a palace, the gates of which were open and fixed back to the wall with large nails. I asked the reason, and was told that the house had not been shut, night or day, for a hundred years. Strangers may present themselves at any hour, and in whatever number; the master has amply provided for the reception of the men and their animals, and is never happier than when they tarry for some time. Nothing of the kind have I seen in any other country." The magnanimous know very well that they who give time, or money, or shelter, to the stranger—so it be done for love, and not for ostentation—do, as it were, put God under obligation to them, so perfect are the compensations of the universe. In some way the time they seem to lose is redeemed, and the pains they seem to take remunerate themselves. These men fan the flame of human love, and raise the standard of civil virtue among mankind. But hospitality must be for service, and not for show, or it pulls down the host. The brave soul rates itself too high to value itself by the splendor of its table and draperies. It gives what it hath, and all it hath, but its own majesty can lend a better grace to bannocks and fair water than belong to city feasts.

The temperance of the hero proceeds from the same wish to do no dishonor to the worthiness he has. But he loves it for its elegancy, not for its austerity. It seems

not worth his while to be solemn, and denounce with bitterness flesh-eating or wine-drinking, the use of tobacco, or opium, or tea, or silk, or gold. A great man scarcely knows how he dines, how he dresses; but without railing or precision, his living is natural and poetic. John Eliot, the Indian Apostle, drank water, and said of wine,—"It is a noble, generous liquor, and we should be humbly thankful for it, but, as I remember, water was made before it." Better still is the temperance of King David, who poured out on the ground unto the Lord the water which three of his warriors had brought him to drink, at the peril of their lives.

It is told of Brutus, that when he fell on his sword, after the battle of Philippi, he quoted a line of Euripides,—"O virtue! I have followed thee through life, and I find thee at last but a shade." I doubt not the hero is slandered by this report. The heroic soul does not sell its justice and its nobleness. It does not ask to dine nicely, and to sleep warm. The essence of greatness is the perception that virtue is enough. Poverty is its ornament. It does not need plenty, and can very well abide its loss.

But that which takes my fancy most, in the heroic class, is the good-humor and hilarity they exhibit. It is a height to which common duty can very well attain, to suffer and to dare with solemnity. But these rare souls set opinion, success, and life, at so cheap a rate, that they will not soothe their enemies by petitions, or the show of sorrow, but wear their own habitual greatness. Scipio, charged with peculation, refuses to do himself so great a disgrace as to wait for justification, though he had the scroll of his accounts in his hands, but tears it to pieces before the tribunes. Socrates's condemnation of himself to be maintained in all honor in the Prytaneum, during his life, and Sir Thomas More's playfulness at the scaffold, are of the same strain. In Beaumont and Fletcher's "Sea Voyage," Juletta tells the stout captain and his company, —

Jul. Why, slaves, 't is in our power to hang ye.

Master. Very likely,
'T is in our powers, then, to be hanged, and scorn
   ye."

These replies are sound and whole. Sport is the bloom and glow of a perfect health. The great will not condescend to take any thing seriously; all must be as gay as the song of a canary, though it were the building of cities, or the eradication of old and foolish churches and nations, which have cumbered the earth long thousands of years. Simple hearts put all the history and customs of this world behind them, and play their own game in innocent defiance of the Blue-Laws of the

world; and such would appear, could we see the human race assembled in vision, like little children frolicking together; though, to the eyes of mankind at large, they wear a stately and solemn garb of works and influences.

The interest these fine stories have for us, the power of a romance over the boy who grasps the forbidden book under his bench at school, our delight in the hero, is the main fact to our purpose. All these great and transcendent properties are ours. If we dilate in beholding the Greek energy, the Roman pride, it is that we are already domesticating the same sentiment. Let us find room for this great guest in our small houses. The first step of worthiness will be to disabuse us of our superstitious associations with places and times, with number and size. Why should these words, Athenian, Roman, Asia, and England, so tingle in the ear? Where the heart is, there the muses, there the gods sojourn, and not in any geography of fame. Massachusetts, Connecticut River, and Boston Bay, you think paltry places, and the ear loves names of foreign and classic topography. But here we are; and, if we will tarry a little, we may come to learn that here is best. See to it, only, that thyself is here;—and art and nature, hope and fate, friends, angels, and the Supreme Being, shall not be absent from the chamber where thou sittest. Epaminondas, brave and affectionate, does not seem to us to need Olympus to die upon, nor the Syrian

sunshine. He lies very well where he is. The Jerseys were handsome ground enough for Washington to tread, and London streets for the feet of Milton. A great man makes his climate genial in the imagination of men, and its air the beloved element of all delicate spirits. That country is the fairest, which is inhabited by the noblest minds. The pictures which fill the imagination in reading the actions of Pericles, Xenophon, Columbus, Bayard, Sidney, Hampden, teach us how needlessly mean our life is, that we, by the depth of our living, should deck it with more than regal or national splendor, and act on principles that should interest man and nature in the length of our days.

We have seen or heard of many extraordinary young men, who never ripened, or whose performance in actual life was not extraordinary. When we see their air and mien, when we hear them speak of society, of books, of religion, we admire their superiority, they seem to throw contempt on our entire polity and social state; theirs is the tone of a youthful giant, who is sent to work revolutions. But they enter an active profession, and the forming Colossus shrinks to the common size of man. The magic they used was the ideal tendencies, which always make the Actual ridiculous; but the tough world had its revenge the moment they put their horses of the sun to plough in its furrow. They found no example and no companion, and their heart fainted. What then?

The lesson they gave in their first aspirations is yet true; and a better valor and a purer truth shall one day organize their belief. Or why should a woman liken herself to any historical woman, and think, because Sappho, or Sevigne, or De Stael, or the cloistered souls who have had genius and cultivation, do not satisfy the imagination and the serene Themis, none can,— certainly not she. Why not? She has a new and unattempted problem to solve, perchance that of the happiest nature that ever bloomed. Let the maiden, with erect soul, walk serenely on her way, accept the hint of each new experience, search in turn all the objects that solicit her eye, that she may learn the power and the charm of her new-born being, which is the kindling of a new dawn in the recesses of space. The fair girl, who repels interference by a decided and proud choice of influences, so careless of pleasing, so wilful and lofty, inspires every beholder with somewhat of her own nobleness. The silent heart encourages her; O friend, never strike sail to a fear! Come into port greatly, or sail with God the seas. Not in vain you live, for every passing eye is cheered and refined by the vision.

The characteristic of heroism is its persistency. All men have wandering impulses, fits, and starts of generosity. But when you have chosen your part, abide by it, and do not weakly try to reconcile yourself with the world. The heroic cannot be the common, nor the common the

heroic. Yet we have the weakness to expect the sympathy of people in those actions whose excellence is that they outrun sympathy, and appeal to a tardy justice. If you would serve your brother, because it is fit for you to serve him, do not take back your words when you find that prudent people do not commend you. Adhere to your own act, and congratulate yourself if you have done something strange and extravagant, and broken the monotony of a decorous age. It was a high counsel that I once heard given to a young person,—"Always do what you are afraid to do." A simple, manly character need never make an apology, but should regard its past action with the calmness of Phocion, when he admitted that the event of the battle was happy, yet did not regret his dissuasion from the battle.

There is no weakness or exposure for which we cannot find consolation in the thought,—this is a part of my constitution, part of my relation and office to my fellow-creature. Has nature covenanted with me that I should never appear to disadvantage, never make a ridiculous figure? Let us be generous of our dignity, as well as of our money. Greatness once and for ever has done with opinion. We tell our charities, not because we wish to be praised for them, not because we think they have great merit, but for our justification. It is a capital blunder; as you discover, when another man recites his charities.

To speak the truth, even with some austerity, to live with some rigor of temperance, or some extremes of generosity, seems to be an asceticism which common good-nature would appoint to those who are at ease and in plenty, in sign that they feel a brotherhood with the great multitude of suffering men. And not only need we breathe and exercise the soul by assuming the penalties of abstinence, of debt, of solitude, of unpopularity, but it behooves the wise man to look with a bold eye into those rarer dangers which sometimes invade men, and to familiarize himself with disgusting forms of disease, with sounds of execration, and the vision of violent death.

Times of heroism are generally times of terror, but the day never shines in which this element may not work. The circumstances of man, we say, are historically somewhat better in this country, and at this hour, than perhaps ever before. More freedom exists for culture. It will not now run against an axe at the first step out of the beaten track of opinion. But whoso is heroic will always find crises to try his edge. Human virtue demands her champions and martyrs, and the trial of persecution always proceeds. It is but the other day that the brave Lovejoy gave his breast to the bullets of a mob, for the rights of free speech and opinion, and died when it was better not to live.

I see not any road of perfect peace which a man can walk, but after the counsel of his own bosom. Let him quit too much association, let him go home much, and stablish himself in those courses he approves. The unremitting retention of simple and high sentiments in obscure duties is hardening the character to that temper which will work with honor, if need be, in the tumult, or on the scaffold. Whatever outrages have happened to men may befall a man again; and very easily in a republic, if there appear any signs of a decay of religion. Coarse slander, fire, tar and feathers, and the gibbet, the youth may freely bring home to his mind, and with what sweetness of temper he can, and inquire how fast he can fix his sense of duty, braving such penalties, whenever it may please the next newspaper and a sufficient number of his neighbors to pronounce his opinions incendiary.

It may calm the apprehension of calamity in the most susceptible heart to see how quick a bound nature has set to the utmost infliction of malice. We rapidly approach a brink over which no enemy can follow us.

"Let them rave: Thou art quiet in thy grave."

In the gloom of our ignorance of what shall be, in the hour when we are deaf to the higher voices, who does not envy those who have seen safely to an end their manful endeavor? Who that sees the meanness of our politics, but inly congratulates Washington that

he is long already wrapped in his shroud, and for ever safe; that he was laid sweet in his grave, the hope of humanity not yet subjugated in him? Who does not sometimes envy the good and brave, who are no more to suffer from the tumults of the natural world, and await with curious complacency the speedy term of his own conversation with finite nature? And yet the love that will be annihilated sooner than treacherous has already made death impossible, and affirms itself no mortal, but a native of the deeps of absolute and inextinguishable being.

Character

The sun set; but set not his hope:
Stars rose; his faith was earlier up:
Fixed on the enormous galaxy,
Deeper and older seemed his eye:
And matched his sufferance sublime
The taciturnity of time.
He spoke, and words more soft than rain
Brought the Age of Gold again:
His action won such reverence sweet,
As hid all measure of the feat.
Work of his hand
He nor commends nor grieves:
Pleads for itself the fact;
As unrepenting Nature leaves
Her every act.

I have read that those who listened to Lord Chatham
felt that there was something finer in the man, than
anything which he said. It has been complained of our

brilliant English historian of the French Revolution, that when he has told all his facts about Mirabeau, they do not justify his estimate of his genius. The Gracchi, Agis, Cleomenes, and others of Plutarch's heroes, do not in the record of facts equal their own fame. Sir Philip Sidney, the Earl of Essex, Sir Walter Raleigh, are men of great figure, and of few deeds. We cannot find the smallest part of the personal weight of Washington, in the narrative of his exploits. The authority of the name of Schiller is too great for his books. This inequality of the reputation to the works or the anecdotes, is not accounted for by saying that the reverberation is longer than the thunder-clap; but somewhat resided in these men which begot an expectation that outran all their performance. The largest part of their power was latent. This is that which we call Character,—a reserved force which acts directly by presence, and without means. It is conceived of as a certain undemonstrable force, a Familiar or Genius, by whose impulses the man is guided, but whose counsels he cannot impart; which is company for him, so that such men are often solitary, or if they chance to be social, do not need society, but can entertain themselves very well alone. The purest literary talent appears at one time great, at another time small, but character is of a stellar and undiminishable greatness. What others effect by talent or by eloquence, this man accomplishes by some

magnetism. "Half his strength he put not forth." His victories are by demonstration of superiority, and not by crossing of bayonets. He conquers, because his arrival alters the face of affairs. "'O Iole! how did you know that Hercules was a god?" "Because," answered Iole, "I was content the moment my eyes fell on him. When I beheld Theseus, I desired that I might see him offer battle, or at least guide his horses in the chariot-race; but Hercules did not wait for a contest; he conquered whether he stood, or walked, or sat, or whatever thing he did.'" Man, ordinarily a pendant to events, only half attached, and that awkwardly, to the world he lives in, in these examples appears to share the life of things, and to be an expression of the same laws which control the tides and the sun, numbers and quantities.

But to use a more modest illustration, and nearer home, I observe, that in our political elections, where this element, if it appears at all, can only occur in its coarsest form, we sufficiently understand its incomparable rate. The people know that they need in their representative much more than talent, namely, the power to make his talent trusted. They cannot come at their ends by sending to Congress a learned, acute, and fluent speaker, if he be not one, who, before he was appointed by the people to represent them, was appointed by Almighty God to stand for a fact,— invincibly persuaded of that fact in himself,—so that

the most confident and the most violent persons learn that here is resistance on which both impudence and terror are wasted, namely, faith in a fact. The men who carry their points do not need to inquire of their constituents what they should say, but are themselves the country which they represent: nowhere are its emotions or opinions so instant and true as in them; nowhere so pure from a selfish infusion. The constituency at home hearkens to their words, watches the color of their cheek, and therein, as in a glass, dresses its own. Our public assemblies are pretty good tests of manly force. Our frank countrymen of the west and south have a taste for character, and like to know whether the New Englander is a substantial man, or whether the hand can pass through him.

The same motive force appears in trade. There are geniuses in trade, as well as in war, or the state, or letters; and the reason why this or that man is fortunate, is not to be told. It lies in the man: that is all anybody can tell you about it. See him, and you will know as easily why he succeeds, as, if you see Napoleon, you would comprehend his fortune. In the new objects we recognize the old game, the habit of fronting the fact, and not dealing with it at second hand, through the perceptions of somebody else. Nature seems to authorize trade, as soon as you see the natural merchant, who appears not so much a private agent, as her factor and

Minister of Commerce. His natural probity combines with his insight into the fabric of society, to put him above tricks, and he communicates to all his own faith, that contracts are of no private interpretation. The habit of his mind is a reference to standards of natural equity and public advantage; and he inspires respect, and the wish to deal with him, both for the quiet spirit of honor which attends him, and for the intellectual pastime which the spectacle of so much ability affords. This immensely stretched trade, which makes the capes of the Southern Ocean his wharves, and the Atlantic Sea his familiar port, centres in his brain only; and nobody in the universe can make his place good. In his parlor, I see very well that he has been at hard work this morning, with that knitted brow, and that settled humor, which all his desire to be courteous cannot shake off. I see plainly how many firm acts have been done; how many valiant *noes* have this day been spoken, when others would have uttered ruinous *yeas*. I see, with the pride of art, and skill of masterly arithmetic and power of remote combination, the consciousness of being an agent and playfellow of the original laws of the world. He too believes that none can supply him, and that a man must be born to trade, or he cannot learn it.

This virtue draws the mind more, when it appears in action to ends not so mixed. It works with most energy in the smallest companies and in private relations.

In all cases, it is an extraordinary and incomputable agent. The excess of physical strength is paralyzed by it. Higher natures overpower lower ones by affecting them with a certain sleep. The faculties are locked up, and offer no resistance. Perhaps that is the universal law. When the high cannot bring up the low to itself, it benumbs it, as man charms down the resistance of the lower animals. Men exert on each other a similar occult power. How often has the influence of a true master realized all the tales of magic! A river of command seemed to run down from his eyes into all those who beheld him, a torrent of strong sad light, like an Ohio or Danube, which pervaded them with his thoughts, and colored all events with the hue of his mind. "What means did you employ?" was the question asked of the wife of Concini, in regard to her treatment of Mary of Medici; and the answer was, "Only that influence which every strong mind has over a weak one." Cannot Caesar in irons shuffle off the irons, and transfer them to the person of Hippo or Thraso the turnkey? Is an iron handcuff so immutable a bond? Suppose a slaver on the coast of Guinea should take on board a gang of negroes, which should contain persons of the stamp of Toussaint L'Ouverture: or, let us fancy, under these swarthy masks he has a gang of Washingtons in chains. When they arrive at Cuba, will the relative order of the ship's company be the same? Is there nothing

but rope and iron? Is there no love, no reverence? Is there never a glimpse of right in a poor slave-captain's mind; and cannot these be supposed available to break, or elude, or in any manner overmatch the tension of an inch or two of iron ring?

This is a natural power, like light and heat, and all nature cooperates with it. The reason why we feel one man's presence, and do not feel another's, is as simple as gravity. Truth is the summit of being: justice is the application of it to affairs. All individual natures stand in a scale, according to the purity of this element in them. The will of the pure runs down from them into other natures, as water runs down from a higher into a lower vessel. This natural force is no more to be withstood, than any other natural force. We can drive a stone upward for a moment into the air, but it is yet true that all stones will forever fall; and whatever instances can be quoted of unpunished theft, or of a lie which somebody credited, justice must prevail, and it is the privilege of truth to make itself believed. Character is this moral order seen through the medium of an individual nature. An individual is an encloser. Time and space, liberty and necessity, truth and thought, are left at large no longer. Now, the universe is a close or pound. All things exist in the man tinged with the manners of his soul. With what quality is in him, he infuses all nature that he can reach; nor does he tend

to lose himself in vastness, but, at how long a curve soever, all his regards return into his own good at last. He animates all he can, and he sees only what he animates. He encloses the world, as the patriot does his country, as a material basis for his character, and a theatre for action. A healthy soul stands united with the Just and the True, as the magnet arranges itself with the pole, so that he stands to all beholders like a transparent object betwixt them and the sun, and whoso journeys towards the sun, journeys towards that person. He is thus the medium of the highest influence to all who are not on the same level. Thus, men of character are the conscience of the society to which they belong.

The natural measure of this power is the resistance of circumstances. Impure men consider life as it is reflected in opinions, events, and persons. They cannot see the action, until it is done. Yet its moral element pre-existed in the actor, and its quality as right or wrong, it was easy to predict. Everything in nature is bipolar, or has a positive and negative pole. There is a male and a female, a spirit and a fact, a north and a south. Spirit is the positive, the event is the negative. Will is the north, action the south pole. Character may be ranked as having its natural place in the north. It shares the magnetic currents of the system. The feeble souls are drawn to the south or negative pole. They look at the profit or hurt of the action. They never behold a principle until it is lodged in a person. They do not wish to be lovely, but to be loved. The class of character like to hear of their faults: the other class do not like to hear of faults; they worship events; secure to them a fact, a connexion, a certain chain of circumstances, and they will ask no more. The hero sees that the event is ancillary: it must follow *him*. A given order of events has no power to secure to him the satisfaction which the imagination attaches to it; the soul of goodness escapes from any set of circumstances, whilst prosperity belongs to a certain mind, and will introduce that power and victory which is its natural fruit, into any order of events. No change of circumstances can repair a defect of character. We boast our emancipation from many superstitions; but if we have broken any idols, it is through a transfer of the idolatry. What have I gained, that I no longer immolate a bull to Jove, or to Neptune, or a mouse to Hecate; that I do not tremble before the Eumenides, or the Catholic Purgatory, or the Calvinistic Judgment-day,— if I quake at opinion, the public opinion, as we call it; or at the threat of assault, or contumely, or bad neighbors, or poverty, or mutilation, or at the rumor of revolution, or of murder? If I quake, what matters it what I quake at? Our proper vice takes form in one or another shape, according to the sex, age, or temperament of the person, and, if we are capable of fear, will readily find terrors. The covetousness or

the malignity which saddens me, when I ascribe it to society, is my own. I am always environed by myself. On the other part, rectitude is a perpetual victory, celebrated not by cries of joy, but by serenity, which is joy fixed or habitual. It is disgraceful to fly to events for confirmation of our truth and worth. The capitalist does not run every hour to the broker, to coin his advantages into current money of the realm; he is satisfied to read in the quotations of the market, that his stocks have risen. The same transport which the occurrence of the best events in the best order would occasion me, I must learn to taste purer in the perception that my position is every hour meliorated, and does already command those events I desire. That exultation is only to be checked by the foresight of an order of things so excellent, as to throw all our prosperities into the deepest shade.

The face which character wears to me is self-sufficingness. I revere the person who is riches; so that I cannot think of him as alone, or poor, or exiled, or unhappy, or a client, but as perpetual patron, benefactor, and beatified man. Character is centrality, the impossibility of being displaced or overset. A man should give us a sense of mass. Society is frivolous, and shreds its day into scraps, its conversation into ceremonies and escapes. But if I go to see an ingenious man, I shall think myself poorly entertained if he give me nimble pieces of benevolence and etiquette; rather he shall stand stoutly in his place, and let me apprehend, if it were only his resistance; know that I have encountered a new and positive quality;—great refreshment for both of us. It is much, that he does not accept the conventional opinions and practices. That nonconformity will remain a goad and remembrancer, and every inquirer will have to dispose of him, in the first place. There is nothing real or useful that is not a seat of war. Our houses ring with laughter and personal and critical gossip, but it helps little. But the uncivil, unavailable man, who is a problem and a threat to society, whom it cannot let pass in silence, but must either worship or hate,—and to whom all parties feel related, both the leaders of opinion, and the obscure and eccentric,—he helps; he puts America and Europe in the wrong, and destroys the skepticism which says, "man is a doll, let us eat and drink, 'tis the best we can do," by illuminating the untried and unknown. Acquiescence in the establishment, and appeal to the public, indicate infirm faith, heads which are not clear, and which must see a house built, before they can comprehend the plan of it. The wise man not only leaves out of his thought the many, but leaves out the few. Fountains, fountains, the self-moved, the absorbed, the commander because he is commanded, the assured, the primary,—they are good; for these announce the instant presence of supreme power.

Our action should rest mathematically on our substance. In nature, there are no false valuations. A pound of water in the ocean-tempest has no more gravity than in a midsummer pond. All things work exactly according to their quality, and according to their quantity; attempt nothing they cannot do, except man only. He has pretension: he wishes and attempts things beyond his force. I read in a book of English memoirs, "Mr. Fox (afterwards Lord Holland) said, he must have the Treasury; he had served up to it, and would have it."—Xenophon and his Ten Thousand were quite equal to what they attempted, and did it; so equal, that it was not suspected to be a grand and inimitable exploit. Yet there stands that fact unrepeated, a high-water-mark in military history. Many have attempted it since, and not been equal to it. It is only on reality, that any power of action can be based. No institution will be better than the institutor. I knew an amiable and accomplished person who undertook a practical reform, yet I was never able to find in him the enterprise of love he took in hand. He adopted it by ear and by the understanding from the books he had been reading. All his action was tentative, a piece of the city carried out into the fields, and was the city still, and no new fact, and could not inspire enthusiasm. Had there been something latent in the man, a terrible undemonstrated genius agitating and embarrassing his demeanor, we had watched for its

advent. It is not enough that the intellect should see the evils, and their remedy. We shall still postpone our existence, nor take the ground to which we are entitled, whilst it is only a thought, and not a spirit that incites us. We have not yet served up to it.

These are properties of life, and another trait is the notice of incessant growth. Men should be intelligent and earnest. They must also make us feel, that they have a controlling happy future, opening before them, which sheds a splendor on the passing hour. The hero is misconceived and misreported: he cannot therefore wait to unravel any man's blunders: he is again on his road, adding new powers and honors to his domain, and new claims on your heart, which will bankrupt you, if you have loitered about the old things, and have not kept your relation to him, by adding to your wealth. New actions are the only apologies and explanations of old ones, which the noble can bear to offer or to receive. If your friend has displeased you, you shall not sit down to consider it, for he has already lost all memory of the passage, and has doubled his power to serve you, and, ere you can rise up again, will burden you with blessings.

We have no pleasure in thinking of a benevolence that is only measured by its works. Love is inexhaustible, and if its estate is wasted, its granary emptied, still cheers and enriches, and the man, though he sleep, seems to purify the air, and his house to adorn the landscape

and strengthen the laws. People always recognize this difference. We know who is benevolent, by quite other means than the amount of subscription to soup-societies. It is only low merits that can be enumerated. Fear, when your friends say to you what you have done well, and say it through; but when they stand with uncertain timid looks of respect and half-dislike, and must suspend their judgment for years to come, you may begin to hope. Those who live to the future must always appear selfish to those who live to the present. Therefore it was droll in the good Riemer, who has written memoirs of Goethe, to make out a list of his donations and good deeds, as, so many hundred thalers given to Stilling, to Hegel, to Tischbein: a lucrative place found for Professor Voss, a post under the Grand Duke for Herder, a pension for Meyer, two professors recommended to foreign universities, &c. &c. The longest list of specifications of benefit, would look very short. A man is a poor creature, if he is to be measured so. For, all these, of course, are exceptions; and the rule and hodiernal life of a good man is benefaction. The true charity of Goethe is to be inferred from the account he gave Dr. Eckermann, of the way in which he had spent his fortune. "Each bon-mot of mine has cost a purse of gold. Half a million of my own money, the fortune I inherited, my salary, and the large income derived from my writings for fifty years back, have been expended to instruct me in what

I now know. I have besides seen," &c.

I own it is but poor chat and gossip to go to enumerate traits of this simple and rapid power, and we are painting the lightning with charcoal; but in these long nights and vacations, I like to console myself so. Nothing but itself can copy it. A word warm from the heart enriches me. I surrender at discretion. How death-cold is literary genius before this fire of life! These are the touches that reanimate my heavy soul, and give it eyes to pierce the dark of nature. I find, where I thought myself poor, there was I most rich. Thence comes a new intellectual exaltation, to be again rebuked by some new exhibition of character. Strange alternation of attraction and repulsion! Character repudiates intellect, yet excites it; and character passes into thought, is published so, and then is ashamed before new flashes of moral worth.

Character is nature in the highest form. It is of no use to ape it, or to contend with it. Somewhat is possible of resistance, and of persistence, and of creation, to this power, which will foil all emulation.

This masterpiece is best where no hands but nature's have been laid on it. Care is taken that the greatly-destined shall slip up into life in the shade, with no thousand-eyed Athens to watch and blazon every new thought, every blushing emotion of young genius. Two persons lately,—very young children of the most high

God,—have given me occasion for thought. When I explored the source of their sanctity, and charm for the imagination, it seemed as if each answered, 'From my non-conformity: I never listened to your people's law, or to what they call their gospel, and wasted my time. I was content with the simple rural poverty of my own: hence this sweetness: my work never reminds you of that;—is pure of that.' And nature advertises me in such persons, that, in democratic America, she will not be democratized. How cloistered and constitutionally sequestered from the market and from scandal! It was only this morning, that I sent away some wild flowers of these wood-gods. They are a relief from literature,— these fresh draughts from the sources of thought and sentiment; as we read, in an age of polish and criticism, the first lines of written prose and verse of a nation. How captivating is their devotion to their favorite books, whether Aeschylus, Dante, Shakespeare, or Scott, as feeling that they have a stake in that book: who touches that, touches them;—and especially the total solitude of the critic, the Patmos of thought from which he writes, in unconsciousness of any eyes that shall ever read this writing. Could they dream on still, as angels, and not wake to comparisons, and to be flattered! Yet some natures are too good to be spoiled by praise, and wherever the vein of thought reaches down into the profound, there is no danger from vanity. Solemn friends

will warn them of the danger of the head's being turned by the flourish of trumpets, but they can afford to smile. I remember the indignation of an eloquent Methodist at the kind admonitions of a Doctor of Divinity,— 'My friend, a man can neither be praised nor insulted.' But forgive the counsels; they are very natural. I remember the thought which occurred to me when some ingenious and spiritual foreigners came to America, was, Have you been victimized in being brought hither?—or, prior to that, answer me this, 'Are you victimizable?'

As I have said, nature keeps these sovereignties in her own hands, and however pertly our sermons and disciplines would divide some share of credit, and teach that the laws fashion the citizen, she goes her own gait, and puts the wisest in the wrong. She makes very light of gospels and prophets, as one who has a great many more to produce, and no excess of time to spare on any one. There is a class of men, individuals of which appear at long intervals, so eminently endowed with insight and virtue, that they have been unanimously saluted as *divine*, and who seem to be an accumulation of that power we consider. Divine persons are character born, or, to borrow a phrase from Napoleon, they are victory organized. They are usually received with ill-will, because they are new, and because they set a bound to the exaggeration that has been made of the personality of the last divine person. Nature never rhymes her

children, nor makes two men alike. When we see a great man, we fancy a resemblance to some historical person, and predict the sequel of his character and fortune, a result which he is sure to disappoint. None will ever solve the problem of his character according to our prejudice, but only in his own high unprecedented way. Character wants room; must not be crowded on by persons, nor be judged from glimpses got in the press of affairs or on few occasions. It needs perspective, as a great building. It may not, probably does not, form relations rapidly; and we should not require rash explanation, either on the popular ethics, or on our own, of its action.

I look on Sculpture as history. I do not think the Apollo and the Jove impossible in flesh and blood. Every trait which the artist recorded in stone, he had seen in life, and better than his copy. We have seen many counterfeits, but we are born believers in great men. How easily we read in old books, when men were few, of the smallest action of the patriarchs. We require that a man should be so large and columnar in the landscape, that it should deserve to be recorded, that he arose, and girded up his loins, and departed to such a place. The most credible pictures are those of majestic men who prevailed at their entrance, and convinced the senses; as happened to the eastern magian who was sent to test the merits of Zertusht or Zoroaster. When the Yunani

sage arrived at Balkh, the Persians tell us, Gushtasp appointed a day on which the Mobeds of every country should assemble, and a golden chair was placed for the Yunani sage. Then the beloved of Yezdam, the prophet Zertusht, advanced into the midst of the assembly. The Yunani sage, on seeing that chief, said, "This form and this gait cannot lie, and nothing but truth can proceed from them." Plato said, it was impossible not to believe in the children of the gods, "though they should speak without probable or necessary arguments." I should think myself very unhappy in my associates, if I could not credit the best things in history. "John Bradshaw," says Milton, "appears like a consul, from whom the fasces are not to depart with the year; so that not on the tribunal only, but throughout his life, you would regard him as sitting in judgment upon kings." I find it more credible, since it is anterior information, that one man should *know heaven*, as the Chinese say, than that so many men should know the world. "The virtuous prince confronts the gods, without any misgiving. He waits a hundred ages till a sage comes, and does not doubt. He who confronts the gods, without any misgiving, knows heaven; he who waits a hundred ages until a sage comes, without doubting, knows men. Hence the virtuous prince moves, and for ages shows empire the way." But there is no need to seek remote examples. He is a dull observer whose experience has not taught

him the reality and force of magic, as well as of chemistry. The coldest precisian cannot go abroad without encountering inexplicable influences. One man fastens an eye on him, and the graves of the memory render up their dead; the secrets that make him wretched either to keep or to betray, must be yielded;—another, and he cannot speak, and the bones of his body seem to lose their cartilages; the entrance of a friend adds grace, boldness, and eloquence to him; and there are persons, he cannot choose but remember, who gave a transcendant expansion to his thought, and kindled another life in his bosom.

What is so excellent as strict relations of amity, when they spring from this deep root? The sufficient reply to the skeptic, who doubts the power and the furniture of man, is in that possibility of joyful intercourse with persons, which makes the faith and practice of all reasonable men. I know nothing which life has to offer so satisfying as the profound good understanding, which can subsist, after much exchange of good offices, between two virtuous men, each of whom is sure of himself, and sure of his friend. It is a happiness which postpones all other gratifications, and makes politics, and commerce, and churches, cheap. For, when men shall meet as they ought, each a benefactor, a shower of stars, clothed with thoughts, with deeds, with accomplishments, it should be the festival of nature which all

things announce. Of such friendship, love in the sexes is the first symbol, as all other things are symbols of love. Those relations to the best men, which, at one time, we reckoned the romances of youth, become, in the progress of the character, the most solid enjoyment.

If it were possible to live in right relations with men!—if we could abstain from asking anything of them, from asking their praise, or help, or pity, and content us with compelling them through the virtue of the eldest laws! Could we not deal with a few persons,—with one person,—after the unwritten statutes, and make an experiment of their efficacy? Could we not pay our friend the compliment of truth, of silence, of forbearing? Need we be so eager to seek him? If we are related, we shall meet. It was a tradition of the ancient world, that no metamorphosis could hide a god from a god; and there is a Greek verse which runs,

"The Gods are to each other not unknown."

Friends also follow the laws of divine necessity; they gravitate to each other, and cannot otherwise: —

When each the other shall avoid,
Shall each by each be most enjoyed.

Their relation is not made, but allowed. The gods must seat themselves without seneschal in our Olympus, and as they can instal themselves by seniority divine. Society is spoiled, if pains are taken, if the associates are brought a mile to meet. And if it be not society, it is a mischievous, low, degrading jangle, though made up of the best. All the greatness of each is kept back, and every foible in painful activity, as if the Olympians should meet to exchange snuff-boxes.

Life goes headlong. We chase some flying scheme, or we are hunted by some fear or command behind us. But if suddenly we encounter a friend, we pause; our heat and hurry look foolish enough; now pause, now possession, is required, and the power to swell the moment from the resources of the heart. The moment is all, in all noble relations.

A divine person is the prophecy of the mind; a friend is the hope of the heart. Our beatitude waits for the fulfilment of these two in one. The ages are opening this moral force. All force is the shadow or symbol of that. Poetry is joyful and strong, as it draws its inspiration thence. Men write their names on the world, as they are filled with this. History has been mean; our nations have been mobs; we have never seen a man: that divine form we do not yet know, but only the dream and prophecy of such: we do not know the majestic manners which belong to him, which appease and exalt the beholder. We shall one day see that the most private is the most public energy, that quality atones for quantity, and grandeur of character acts in the dark, and succors them who never saw it. What greatness has yet appeared, is beginnings and encouragements to us in this direction. The history of those gods and saints which the world has written, and then worshipped, are documents of character. The ages have exulted in the manners of a youth who owed nothing to fortune, and who was hanged at the Tyburn of his nation, who, by the pure quality of his nature, shed an epic splendor around the facts of his death, which has transfigured every particular into an universal symbol for the eyes of mankind. This great defeat is hitherto our highest fact. But the mind requires a victory to the senses, a force of character which will convert judge, jury, soldier, and king; which will rule animal and mineral virtues, and blend with the courses of sap, of rivers, of winds, of stars, and of moral agents.

If we cannot attain at a bound to these grandeurs, at least, let us do them homage. In society, high advantages are set down to the possessor, as disadvantages. It requires the more wariness in our private estimates. I do not forgive in my friends the failure to know a fine character, and to entertain it with thankful hospitality. When, at last, that which we have always longed for, is arrived, and shines on us with glad rays

out of that far celestial land, then to be coarse, then to be critical, and treat such a visitant with the jabber and suspicion of the streets, argues a vulgarity that seems to shut the doors of heaven. This is confusion, this the right insanity, when the soul no longer knows its own, nor where its allegiance, its religion, are due. Is there any religion but this, to know, that, wherever in the wide desert of being, the holy sentiment we cherish has opened into a flower, it blooms for me? if none sees it, I see it; I am aware, if I alone, of the greatness of the fact. Whilst it blooms, I will keep sabbath or holy time, and suspend my gloom, and my folly and jokes. Nature is indulged by the presence of this guest. There are many eyes that can detect and honor the prudent and household virtues; there are many that can discern Genius on his starry track, though the mob is incapable; but when that love which is all-suffering, all-abstaining, all-aspiring, which has vowed to itself, that it will be a wretch and also a fool in this world, sooner than soil its white hands by any compliances, comes into our streets and houses,—only the pure and aspiring can know its face, and the only compliment they can pay it, is to own it.

Manners

"How near to good is what is fair!
Which we no sooner see,
But with the lines and outward air
Our senses taken be.
Again yourselves compose,
And now put all the aptness on
Of Figure, that Proportion
Or Color can disclose;
That if those silent arts were lost,
Design and Picture, they might boast
From you a newer ground,
Instructed by the heightening sense
Of dignity and reverence
In their true motions found."

Ben Jonson

Half the world, it is said, knows not how the other half live. Our Exploring Expedition saw the Feejee islanders getting their dinner off human bones;

and they are said to eat their own wives and children. The husbandry of the modern inhabitants of Gournou (west of old Thebes) is philosophical to a fault. To set up their housekeeping, nothing is requisite but two or three earthern pots, a stone to grind meal, and a mat which is the bed. The house, namely, a tomb, is ready without rent or taxes. No rain can pass through the roof, and there is no door, for there is no want of one, as there is nothing to lose. If the house do not please them, they walk out and enter another, as there are several hundreds at their command. "It is somewhat singular," adds Belzoni, to whom we owe this account, "to talk of happiness among people who live in sepulchres, among the corpses and rags of an ancient nation which they know nothing of." In the deserts of Borgoo, the rock-Tibboos still dwell in caves, like cliff-swallows, and the language of these negroes is compared by their neighbors to the shrieking of bats, and to the whistling of birds. Again, the Bornoos have no proper names; individuals are called after their height, thickness, or other accidental quality, and have nicknames merely. But the salt, the dates, the ivory, and the gold, for which these horrible regions are visited, find their way into countries, where the purchaser and consumer can hardly be ranked in one race with these cannibals and man-stealers; countries where man serves himself with metals, wood, stone, glass, gum, cotton,

silk, and wool; honors himself with architecture; writes laws, and contrives to execute his will through the hands of many nations; and, especially, establishes a select society, running through all the countries of intelligent men, a self-constituted aristocracy, or fraternity of the best, which, without written law or exact usage of any kind, perpetuates itself, colonizes every new-planted island, and adopts and makes its own whatever personal beauty or extraordinary native endowment anywhere appears.

What fact more conspicuous in modern history, than the creation of the gentleman? Chivalry is that, and loyalty is that, and, in English literature, half the drama, and all the novels, from Sir Philip Sidney to Sir Walter Scott, paint this figure. The word *gentleman*, which, like the word Christian, must hereafter characterize the present and the few preceding centuries, by the importance attached to it, is a homage to personal and incommunicable properties. Frivolous and fantastic additions have got associated with the name, but the steady interest of mankind in it must be attributed to the valuable properties which it designates. An element which unites all the most forcible persons of every country; makes them intelligible and agreeable to each other, and is somewhat so precise, that it is at once felt if an individual lack the masonic sign, cannot be any casual product, but must be an average result of the

character and faculties universally found in men. It seems a certain permanent average; as the atmosphere is a permanent composition, whilst so many gases are combined only to be decompounded. *Comme il faut*, is the Frenchman's description of good society, *as we must be*. It is a spontaneous fruit of talents and feelings of precisely that class who have most vigor, who take the lead in the world of this hour, and, though far from pure, far from constituting the gladdest and highest tone of human feeling, is as good as the whole society permits it to be. It is made of the spirit, more than of the talent of men, and is a compound result, into which every great force enters as an ingredient, namely, virtue, wit, beauty, wealth, and power.

There is something equivocal in all the words in use to express the excellence of manners and social cultivation, because the quantities are fluxional, and the last effect is assumed by the senses as the cause. The word *gentleman* has not any correlative abstract to express the quality. *Gentility* is mean, and *gentilesse* is obsolete. But we must keep alive in the vernacular, the distinction between *fashion*, a word of narrow and often sinister meaning, and the heroic character which the gentleman imports. The usual words, however, must be respected: they will be found to contain the root of the matter. The point of distinction in all this class of names, as courtesy, chivalry, fashion, and the like, is, that the flower

and fruit, not the grain of the tree, are contemplated. It is beauty which is the aim this time, and not worth. The result is now in question, although our words intimate well enough the popular feeling, that the appearance supposes a substance. The gentleman is a man of truth, lord of his own actions, and expressing that lordship in his behavior, not in any manner dependent and servile either on persons, or opinions, or possessions. Beyond this fact of truth and real force, the word denotes good-nature or benevolence: manhood first, and then gentleness. The popular notion certainly adds a condition of ease and fortune; but that is a natural result of personal force and love, that they should possess and dispense the goods of the world. In times of violence, every eminent person must fall in with many opportunities to approve his stoutness and worth; therefore every man's name that emerged at all from the mass in the feudal ages, rattles in our ear like a flourish of trumpets. But personal force never goes out of fashion. That is still paramount today, and, in the moving crowd of good society, the men of valor and reality are known, and rise to their natural place. The competition is transferred from war to politics and trade, but the personal force appears readily enough in these new arenas.

Power first, or no leading class. In politics and in trade, bruisers and pirates are of better promise than talkers and clerks. God knows that all sorts of gentlemen

knock at the door; but whenever used in strictness, and with any emphasis, the name will be found to point at original energy. It describes a man standing in his own right, and working after untaught methods. In a good lord, there must first be a good animal, at least to the extent of yielding the incomparable advantage of animal spirits. The ruling class must have more, but they must have these, giving in every company the sense of power, which makes things easy to be done which daunt the wise. The society of the energetic class, in their friendly and festive meetings, is full of courage, and of attempts, which intimidate the pale scholar. The courage which girls exhibit is like a battle of Lundy's Lane, or a sea-fight. The intellect relies on memory to make some supplies to face these extemporaneous squadrons. But memory is a base mendicant with basket and badge, in the presence of these sudden masters. The rulers of society must be up to the work of the world, and equal to their versatile office: men of the right Caesarian pattern, who have great range of affinity. I am far from believing the timid maxim of Lord Falkland, ("that for ceremony there must go two to it; since a bold fellow will go through the cunningest forms,") and am of opinion that the gentleman is the bold fellow whose forms are not to be broken through; and only that plenteous nature is rightful master, which is the complement of whatever person it converses with. My

gentleman gives the law where he is; he will outpray saints in chapel, outgeneral veterans in the field, and outshine all courtesy in the hall. He is good company for pirates, and good with academicians; so that it is useless to fortify yourself against him; he has the private entrance to all minds, and I could as easily exclude myself, as him. The famous gentlemen of Asia and Europe have been of this strong type: Saladin, Sapor, the Cid, Julius Caesar, Scipio, Alexander, Pericles, and the lordliest personages. They sat very carelessly in their chairs, and were too excellent themselves, to value any condition at a high rate.

A plentiful fortune is reckoned necessary, in the popular judgment, to the completion of this man of the world: and it is a material deputy which walks through the dance which the first has led. Money is not essential, but this wide affinity is, which transcends the habits of clique and caste, and makes itself felt by men of all classes. If the aristocrat is only valid in fashionable circles, and not with truckmen, he will never be a leader in fashion; and if the man of the people cannot speak on equal terms with the gentleman, so that the gentleman shall perceive that he is already really of his own order, he is not to be feared. Diogenes, Socrates, and Epaminondas, are gentlemen of the best blood, who have chosen the condition of poverty, when that of wealth was equally open to them. I use these

old names, but the men I speak of are my contemporaries. Fortune will not supply to every generation one of these well-appointed knights, but every collection of men furnishes some example of the class: and the politics of this country, and the trade of every town, are controlled by these hardy and irresponsible doers, who have invention to take the lead, and a broad sympathy which puts them in fellowship with crowds, and makes their action popular.

The manners of this class are observed and caught with devotion by men of taste. The association of these masters with each other, and with men intelligent of their merits, is mutually agreeable and stimulating. The good forms, the happiest expressions of each, are repeated and adopted. By swift consent, everything superfluous is dropped, everything graceful is renewed. Fine manners show themselves formidable to the uncultivated man. They are a subtler science of defence to parry and intimidate; but once matched by the skill of the other party, they drop the point of the sword,— points and fences disappear, and the youth finds himself in a more transparent atmosphere, wherein life is a less troublesome game, and not a misunderstanding rises between the players. Manners aim to facilitate life, to get rid of impediments, and bring the man pure to energize. They aid our dealing and conversation, as a railway aids travelling, by getting rid of all avoidable

obstructions of the road, and leaving nothing to be conquered but pure space. These forms very soon become fixed, and a fine sense of propriety is cultivated with the more heed, that it becomes a badge of social and civil distinctions. Thus grows up Fashion, an equivocal semblance, the most puissant, the most fantastic and frivolous, the most feared and followed, and which morals and violence assault in vain.

There exists a strict relation between the class of power, and the exclusive and polished circles. The last are always filled or filling from the first. The strong men usually give some allowance even to the petulances of fashion, for that affinity they find in it. Napoleon, child of the revolution, destroyer of the old noblesse, never ceased to court the Faubourg St. Germain: doubtless with the feeling, that fashion is a homage to men of his stamp. Fashion, though in a strange way, represents all manly virtue. It is virtue gone to seed: it is a kind of posthumous honor. It does not often caress the great, but the children of the great: it is a hall of the Past. It usually sets its face against the great of this hour. Great men are not commonly in its halls: they are absent in the field: they are working, not triumphing. Fashion is made up of their children; of those, who, through the value and virtue of somebody, have acquired lustre to their name, marks of distinction, means of cultivation and generosity, and, in their physical organ-

ization, a certain health and excellence, which secures
to them, if not the highest power to work, yet high
power to enjoy. The class of power, the working heroes,
the Cortez, the Nelson, the Napoleon, see that this is
the festivity and permanent celebration of such as they;
that fashion is funded talent; is Mexico, Marengo, and
Trafalgar beaten out thin; that the brilliant names of
fashion run back to just such busy names as their own,
fifty or sixty years ago. They are the sowers, their sons
shall be the reapers, and *their* sons, in the ordinary
course of things, must yield the possession of the harvest
to new competitors with keener eyes and stronger
frames. The city is recruited from the country. In the
year 1805, it is said, every legitimate monarch in Europe
was imbecile. The city would have died out, rotted, and
exploded, long ago, but that it was reinforced from the
fields. It is only country which came to town day before
yesterday, that is city and court today.

Aristocracy and fashion are certain inevitable results.
These mutual selections are indestructible. If they
provoke anger in the least favored class, and the excluded
majority revenge themselves on the excluding minority,
by the strong hand, and kill them, at once a new class
finds itself at the top, as certainly as cream rises in a
bowl of milk: and if the people should destroy class after
class, until two men only were left, one of these would
be the leader, and would be involuntarily served and

copied by the other. You may keep this minority out of sight and out of mind, but it is tenacious of life, and is one of the estates of the realm. I am the more struck with this tenacity, when I see its work. It respects the administration of such unimportant matters, that we should not look for any durability in its rule. We sometimes meet men under some strong moral influence, as, a patriotic, a literary, a religious movement, and feel that the moral sentiment rules man and nature. We think all other distinctions and ties will be slight and fugitive, this of caste or fashion, for example; yet come from year to year, and see how permanent that is, in this Boston or New York life of man, where, too, it has not the least countenance from the law of the land. Not in Egypt or in India a firmer or more impassable line. Here are associations whose ties go over, and under, and through it, a meeting of merchants, a military corps, a college-class, a fire-club, a professional association, a political, a religious convention;—the persons seem to draw inseparably near; yet, that assembly once dispersed, its members will not in the year meet again. Each returns to his degree in the scale of good society, porcelain remains porcelain, and earthen earthen. The objects of fashion may be frivolous, or fashion may be objectless, but the nature of this union and selection can be neither frivolous nor accidental. Each man's rank in that perfect graduation depends on some symmetry in his structure,

or some agreement in his structure to the symmetry of society. Its doors unbar instantaneously to a natural claim of their own kind. A natural gentleman finds his way in, and will keep the oldest patrician out, who has lost his intrinsic rank. Fashion understands itself; good-breeding and personal superiority of whatever country readily fraternize with those of every other. The chiefs of savage tribes have distinguished themselves in London and Paris, by the purity of their tournure.

To say what good of fashion we can,—it rests on reality, and hates nothing so much as pretenders;—to exclude and mystify pretenders, and send them into everlasting 'Coventry,' is its delight. We contemn, in turn, every other gift of men of the world; but the habit even in little and the least matters, of not appealing to any but our own sense of propriety, constitutes the foundation of all chivalry. There is almost no kind of self-reliance, so it be sane and proportioned, which fashion does not occasionally adopt, and give it the freedom of its saloons. A sainted soul is always elegant, and, if it will, passes unchallenged into the most guarded ring. But so will Jock the teamster pass, in some crisis that brings him thither, and find favor, as long as his head is not giddy with the new circumstance, and the iron shoes do not wish to dance in waltzes and cotillons. For there is nothing settled in manners, but the laws of behavior yield to the energy of the individual. The

maiden at her first ball, the country-man at a city dinner, believes that there is a ritual according to which every act and compliment must be performed, or the failing party must be cast out of this presence. Later, they learn that good sense and character make their own forms every moment, and speak or abstain, take wine or refuse it, stay or go, sit in a chair or sprawl with children on the floor, or stand on their head, or what else soever, in a new and aboriginal way: and that strong will is always in fashion, let who will be unfashionable. All that fashion demands is composure, and self-content. A circle of men perfectly well-bred would be a company of sensible persons, in which every man's native manners and character appeared. If the fashionist have not this quality, he is nothing. We are such lovers of self-reliance, that we excuse in a man many sins, if he will show us a complete satisfaction in his position, which asks no leave to be, of mine, or any man's good opinion. But any deference to some eminent man or woman of the world, forfeits all privilege of nobility. He is an underling: I have nothing to do with him; I will speak with his master. A man should not go where he cannot carry his whole sphere or society with him,—not bodily, the whole circle of his friends, but atmospherically. He should preserve in a new company the same attitude of mind and reality of relation, which his daily associates draw him to, else he is shorn of his best beams, and

will be an orphan in the merriest club. "If you could see Vich Ian Vohr with his tail on!—" But Vich Ian Vohr must always carry his belongings in some fashion, if not added as honor, then severed as disgrace.

There will always be in society certain persons who are mercuries of its approbation, and whose glance will at any time determine for the curious their standing in the world. These are the chamberlains of the lesser gods. Accept their coldness as an omen of grace with the loftier deities, and allow them all their privilege. They are clear in their office, nor could they be thus formidable, without their own merits. But do not measure the importance of this class by their pretension, or imagine that a fop can be the dispenser of honor and shame. They pass also at their just rate; for how can they otherwise, in circles which exist as a sort of herald's office for the sifting of character?

As the first thing man requires of man, is reality, so, that appears in all the forms of society. We pointedly, and by name, introduce the parties to each other. Know you before all heaven and earth, that this is Andrew, and this is Gregory;—they look each other in the eye; they grasp each other's hand, to identify and signalize each other. It is a great satisfaction. A gentleman never dodges: his eyes look straight forward, and he assures the other party, first of all, that he has been met. For what is it that we seek, in so many visits and hospitalities? Is it your draperies, pictures, and decorations? Or, do we not insatiably ask, Was a man in the house? I may easily go into a great household where there is much substance, excellent provision for comfort, luxury, and taste, and yet not encounter there any Amphitryon, who shall subordinate these appendages. I may go into a cottage, and find a farmer who feels that he is the man I have come to see, and fronts me accordingly. It was therefore a very natural point of old feudal etiquette, that a gentleman who received a visit, though it were of his sovereign, should not leave his roof, but should wait his arrival at the door of his house. No house, though it were the Thuilleries, or the Escurial, is good for anything without a master. And yet we are not often gratified by this hospitality. Every body we know surrounds himself with a fine house, fine books, conservatory, gardens, equipage, and all manner of toys, as screens to interpose between himself and his guest. Does it not seem as if man was of a very sly, elusive nature, and dreaded nothing so much as a full rencontre front to front with his fellow? It were unmerciful, I know, quite to abolish the use of these screens, which are of eminent convenience, whether the guest is too great, or too little. We call together many friends who keep each other in play, or, by luxuries and ornaments we amuse the young people, and guard our retirement. Or if, perchance, a searching realist comes to our gate,

before whose eye we have no care to stand, then again we run to our curtain, and hide ourselves as Adam at the voice of the Lord God in the garden. Cardinal Caprara, the Pope's legate at Paris, defended himself from the glances of Napoleon, by an immense pair of green spectacles. Napoleon remarked them, and speedily managed to rally them off: and yet Napoleon, in his turn, was not great enough with eight hundred thousand troops at his back, to face a pair of freeborn eyes, but fenced himself with etiquette, and within triple barriers of reserve: and, as all the world knows from Madame de Stael, was wont, when he found himself observed, to discharge his face of all expression. But emperors and rich men are by no means the most skilful masters of good manners. No rentroll nor army-list can dignify skulking and dissimulation: and the first point of courtesy must always be truth, as really all the forms of good-breeding point that way.

I have just been reading, in Mr. Hazlitt's translation, Montaigne's account of his journey into Italy, and am struck with nothing more agreeably than the self-respecting fashions of the time. His arrival in each place, the arrival of a gentleman of France, is an event of some consequence. Wherever he goes, he pays a visit to whatever prince or gentleman of note resides upon his road, as a duty to himself and to civilization. When he leaves any house in which he has lodged for a few weeks, he causes his arms to be painted and hung up as a perpetual sign to the house, as was the custom of gentlemen.

The complement of this graceful self-respect, and that of all the points of good breeding I most require and insist upon, is deference. I like that every chair should be a throne, and hold a king. I prefer a tendency to stateliness, to an excess of fellowship. Let the incommunicable objects of nature and the metaphysical isolation of man teach us independence. Let us not be too much acquainted. I would have a man enter his house through a hall filled with heroic and sacred sculptures, that he might not want the hint of tranquillity and self-poise. We should meet each morning, as from foreign countries, and spending the day together, should depart at night, as into foreign countries. In all things I would have the island of a man inviolate. Let us sit apart as the gods, talking from peak to peak all round Olympus. No degree of affection need invade this religion. This is myrrh and rosemary to keep the other sweet. Lovers should guard their strangeness. If they forgive too much, all slides into confusion and meanness. It is easy to push this deference to a Chinese etiquette; but coolness and absence of heat and haste indicate fine qualities. A gentleman makes no noise: a lady is serene. Proportionate is our disgust at those invaders who fill a studious house with blast and running, to secure some paltry convenience. Not less I dislike a

low sympathy of each with his neighbor's needs. Must we have a good understanding with one another's palates? as foolish people who have lived long together, know when each wants salt or sugar. I pray my companion, if he wishes for bread, to ask me for bread, and if he wishes for sassafras or arsenic, to ask me for them, and not to hold out his plate, as if I knew already. Every natural function can be dignified by deliberation and privacy. Let us leave hurry to slaves. The compliments and ceremonies of our breeding should signify, however remotely, the recollection of the grandeur of our destiny.

The flower of courtesy does not very well bide handling, but if we dare to open another leaf, and explore what parts go to its conformation, we shall find also an intellectual quality. To the leaders of men, the brain as well as the flesh and the heart must furnish a proportion. Defect in manners is usually the defect of fine perceptions. Men are too coarsely made for the delicacy of beautiful carriage and customs. It is not quite sufficient to good-breeding, a union of kindness and independence. We imperatively require a perception of, and a homage to beauty in our companions. Other virtues are in request in the field and workyard, but a certain degree of taste is not to be spared in those we sit with. I could better eat with one who did not respect the truth or the laws, than with a sloven and unpresentable person.

Moral qualities rule the world, but at short distances, the senses are despotic. The same discrimination of fit and fair runs out, if with less rigor, into all parts of life. The average spirit of the energetic class is good sense, acting under certain limitations and to certain ends. It entertains every natural gift. Social in its nature, it respects everything which tends to unite men. It delights in measure. The love of beauty is mainly the love of measure or proportion. The person who screams, or uses the superlative degree, or converses with heat, puts whole drawing-rooms to flight. If you wish to be loved, love measure. You must have genius, or a prodigious usefulness, if you will hide the want of measure. This perception comes in to polish and perfect the parts of the social instrument. Society will pardon much to genius and special gifts, but, being in its nature a convention, it loves what is conventional, or what belongs to coming together. That makes the good and bad of manners, namely, what helps or hinders fellowship. For, fashion is not good sense absolute, but relative; not good sense private, but good sense entertaining company. It hates corners and sharp points of character, hates quarrelsome, egotistical, solitary, and gloomy people; hates whatever can interfere with total blending of parties; whilst it values all peculiarities as in the highest degree refreshing, which can consist with good fellowship. And besides the general infusion of wit to

heighten civility, the direct splendor of intellectual power is ever welcome in fine society as the costliest addition to its rule and its credit.

The dry light must shine in to adorn our festival, but it must be tempered and shaded, or that will also offend. Accuracy is essential to beauty, and quick perceptions to politeness, but not too quick perceptions. One may be too punctual and too precise. He must leave the omniscience of business at the door, when he comes into the palace of beauty. Society loves creole natures, and sleepy, languishing manners, so that they cover sense, grace, and good-will; the air of drowsy strength, which disarms criticism; perhaps, because such a person seems to reserve himself for the best of the game, and not spend himself on surfaces; an ignoring eye, which does not see the annoyances, shifts, and inconveniences, that cloud the brow and smother the voice of the sensitive.

Therefore, besides personal force and so much perception as constitutes unerring taste, society demands in its patrician class, another element already intimated, which it significantly terms good-nature, expressing all degrees of generosity, from the lowest willingness and faculty to oblige, up to the heights of magnanimity and love. Insight we must have, or we shall run against one another, and miss the way to our food; but intellect is selfish and barren. The secret of success in society, is a certain heartiness and sympathy. A man who is not happy in the company, cannot find any word in his memory that will fit the occasion. All his information is a little impertinent. A man who is happy there, finds in every turn of the conversation equally lucky occasions for the introduction of that which he has to say. The favorites of society, and what it calls *whole souls*, are able men, and of more spirit than wit, who have no uncomfortable egotism, but who exactly fill the hour and the company, contented and contenting, at a marriage or a funeral, a ball or a jury, a water-party or a shooting-match. England, which is rich in gentlemen, furnished, in the beginning of the present century, a good model of that genius which the world loves, in Mr. Fox, who added to his great abilities the most social disposition, and real love of men. Parliamentary history has few better passages than the debate, in which Burke and Fox separated in the House of Commons; when Fox urged on his old friend the claims of old friendship with such tenderness, that the house was moved to tears. Another anecdote is so close to my matter, that I must hazard the story. A tradesman who had long dunned him for a note of three hundred guineas, found him one day counting gold, and demanded payment: "No," said Fox, "I owe this money to Sheridan: it is a debt of honor: if an accident should happen to me, he has nothing to show." "Then," said the creditor, "I change

my debt into a debt of honor," and tore the note in pieces. Fox thanked the man for his confidence, and paid him, saying, "his debt was of older standing, and Sheridan must wait." Lover of liberty, friend of the Hindoo, friend of the African slave, he possessed a great personal popularity; and Napoleon said of him on the occasion of his visit to Paris, in 1805, "Mr. Fox will always hold the first place in an assembly at the Thuilleries."

We may easily seem ridiculous in our eulogy of courtesy, whenever we insist on benevolence as its foundation. The painted phantasm Fashion rises to cast a species of derision on what we say. But I will neither be driven from some allowance to Fashion as a symbolic institution, nor from the belief that love is the basis of courtesy. We must obtain *that*, if we can; but by all means we must affirm *this*. Life owes much of its spirit to these sharp contrasts. Fashion which affects to be honor, is often, in all men's experience, only a ballroom-code. Yet, so long as it is the highest circle, in the imagination of the best heads on the planet, there is something necessary and excellent in it; for it is not to be supposed that men have agreed to be the dupes of anything preposterous; and the respect which these mysteries inspire in the most rude and sylvan characters, and the curiosity with which details of high life are read, betray the universality of the love of cultivated manners.

I know that a comic disparity would be felt, if we should enter the acknowledged 'first circles,' and apply these terrific standards of justice, beauty, and benefit, to the individuals actually found there. Monarchs and heroes, sages and lovers, these gallants are not. Fashion has many classes and many rules of probation and admission; and not the best alone. There is not only the right of conquest, which genius pretends,—the individual, demonstrating his natural aristocracy best of the best;— but less claims will pass for the time; for Fashion loves lions, and points, like Circe, to her horned company. This gentleman is this afternoon arrived from Denmark; and that is my Lord Ride, who came yesterday from Bagdat; here is Captain Friese, from Cape Turnagain; and Captain Symmes, from the interior of the earth; and Monsieur Jovaire, who came down this morning in a balloon; Mr. Hobnail, the reformer; and Reverend Jul Bat, who has converted the whole torrid zone in his Sunday school; and Signor Torre del Greco, who extinguished Vesuvius by pouring into it the Bay of Naples; Spahi, the Persian ambassador; and Tul Wil Shan, the exiled nabob of Nepaul, whose saddle is the new moon.—But these are monsters of one day, and tomorrow will be dismissed to their holes and dens; for, in these rooms, every chair is waited for. The artist, the scholar, and, in general, the clerisy, wins its way up into these places, and gets represented here, somewhat on

this footing of conquest. Another mode is to pass through all the degrees, spending a year and a day in St. Michael's Square, being steeped in Cologne water, and perfumed, and dined, and introduced, and properly grounded in all the biography, and politics, and anecdotes of the boudoirs.

Yet these fineries may have grace and wit. Let there be grotesque sculpture about the gates and offices of temples. Let the creed and commandments even have the saucy homage of parody. The forms of politeness universally express benevolence in superlative degrees. What if they are in the mouths of selfish men, and used as means of selfishness? What if the false gentleman almost bows the true out of the world? What if the false gentleman contrives so to address his companion, as civilly to exclude all others from his discourse, and also to make them feel excluded? Real service will not lose its nobleness. All generosity is not merely French and sentimental; nor is it to be concealed, that living blood and a passion of kindness does at last distinguish God's gentleman from Fashion's. The epitaph of Sir Jenkin Grout is not wholly unintelligible to the present age. "Here lies Sir Jenkin Grout, who loved his friend, and persuaded his enemy: what his mouth ate, his hand paid for: what his servants robbed, he restored: if a woman gave him pleasure, he supported her in pain: he never forgot his children: and whoso touched his

finger, drew after it his whole body." Even the line of heroes is not utterly extinct. There is still ever some admirable person in plain clothes, standing on the wharf, who jumps in to rescue a drowning man; there is still some absurd inventor of charities; some guide and comforter of runaway slaves; some friend of Poland; some Philhellene; some fanatic who plants shade-trees for the second and third generation, and orchards when he is grown old; some well-concealed piety; some just man happy in an ill-fame; some youth ashamed of the favors of fortune, and impatiently casting them on other shoulders. And these are the centres of society, on which it returns for fresh impulses. These are the creators of Fashion, which is an attempt to organize beauty of behavior. The beautiful and the generous are, in the theory, the doctors and apostles of this church: Scipio, and the Cid, and Sir Philip Sidney, and Washington, and every pure and valiant heart, who worshipped Beauty by word and by deed. The persons who constitute the natural aristocracy, are not found in the actual aristocracy, or, only on its edge; as the chemical energy of the spectrum is found to be greatest just outside of the spectrum. Yet that is the infirmity of the seneschals, who do not know their sovereign, when he appears. The theory of society supposes the existence and sovereignty of these. It divines afar off their coming. It says with the elder gods, —

"As Heaven and Earth are fairer far Than Chaos
and blank Darkness, though once chiefs; And as
we show beyond that Heaven and Earth, In form
and shape compact and beautiful; So, on our heels
a fresh perfection treads; A power, more strong
in beauty, born of us, And fated to excel us, as
we pass In glory that old Darkness: ————— for,
't is the eternal law, That first in beauty shall be
first in might."

Therefore, within the ethnical circle of good society,
there is a narrower and higher circle, concentration of
its light, and flower of courtesy, to which there is always
a tacit appeal of pride and reference, as to its inner and
imperial court, the parliament of love and chivalry. And
this is constituted of those persons in whom heroic
dispositions are native, with the love of beauty, the
delight in society, and the power to embellish the passing
day. If the individuals who compose the purest circles
of aristocracy in Europe, the guarded blood of centuries,
should pass in review, in such manner as that we could,
at leisure, and critically inspect their behavior, we might
find no gentleman, and no lady; for, although excellent
specimens of courtesy and high-breeding would gratify
us in the assemblage, in the particulars, we should detect
offence. Because, elegance comes of no breeding, but
of birth. There must be romance of character, or the

most fastidious exclusion of impertinencies will not avail. It must be genius which takes that direction: it must be not courteous, but courtesy. High behavior is as rare in fiction, as it is in fact. Scott is praised for the fidelity with which he painted the demeanor and conversation of the superior classes. Certainly, kings and queens, nobles and great ladies, had some right to complain of the absurdity that had been put in their mouths, before the days of Waverley; but neither does Scott's dialogue bear criticism. His lords brave each other in smart epigramatic speeches, but the dialogue is in costume, and does not please on the second reading: it is not warm with life. In Shakespeare alone, the speakers do not strut and bridle, the dialogue is easily great, and he adds to so many titles that of being the best-bred man in England, and in Christendom. Once or twice in a lifetime we are permitted to enjoy the charm of noble manners, in the presence of a man or woman who have no bar in their nature, but whose character emanates freely in their word and gesture. A beautiful form is better than a beautiful face; a beautiful behavior is better than a beautiful form: it gives a higher pleasure than statues or pictures; it is the finest of the fine arts. A man is but a little thing in the midst of the objects of nature, yet, by the moral quality radiating from his countenance, he may abolish all considerations of magnitude, and in his manners equal the majesty of the

world. I have seen an individual, whose manners, though wholly within the conventions of elegant society, were never learned there, but were original and commanding, and held out protection and prosperity; one who did not need the aid of a court-suit, but carried the holiday in his eye; who exhilarated the fancy by flinging wide the doors of new modes of existence; who shook off the captivity of etiquette, with happy, spirited bearing, good-natured and free as Robin Hood; yet with the port of an emperor,—if need be, calm, serious, and fit to stand the gaze of millions.

The open air and the fields, the street and public chambers, are the places where Man executes his will; let him yield or divide the sceptre at the door of the house. Woman, with her instinct of behavior, instantly detects in man a love of trifles, any coldness or imbecility, or, in short, any want of that large, flowing, and magnanimous deportment, which is indispensable as an exterior in the hall. Our American institutions have been friendly to her, and at this moment, I esteem it a chief felicity of this country, that it excels in women. A certain awkward consciousness of inferiority in the men, may give rise to the new chivalry in behalf of Woman's Rights. Certainly, let her be as much better placed in the laws and in social forms, as the most zealous reformer can ask, but I confide so entirely in her inspiring and musical nature, that I believe only herself can show us

how she shall be served. The wonderful generosity of her sentiments raises her at times into heroical and godlike regions, and verifies the pictures of Minerva, Juno, or Polymnia; and, by the firmness with which she treads her upward path, she convinces the coarsest calculators that another road exists, than that which their feet know. But besides those who make good in our imagination the place of muses and of Delphic Sibyls, are there not women who fill our vase with wine and roses to the brim, so that the wine runs over and fills the house with perfume; who inspire us with courtesy; who unloose our tongues, and we speak; who anoint our eyes, and we see? We say things we never thought to have said; for once, our walls of habitual reserve vanished, and left us at large; we were children playing with children in a wide field of flowers. Steep us, we cried, in these influences, for days, for weeks, and we shall be sunny poets, and will write out in many-colored words the romance that you are. Was it Hafiz or Firdousi that said of his Persian Lilla, She was an elemental force, and astonished me by her amount of life, when I saw her day after day radiating, every instant, redundant joy and grace on all around her. She was a solvent powerful to reconcile all heterogeneous persons into one society: like air or water, an element of such a great range of affinities, that it combines readily with a thousand substances. Where she is present, all others will be more

than they are wont. She was a unit and whole, so that whatsoever she did, became her. She had too much sympathy and desire to please, than that you could say, her manners were marked with dignity, yet no princess could surpass her clear and erect demeanor on each occasion. She did not study the Persian grammar, nor the books of the seven poets, but all the poems of the seven seemed to be written upon her. For, though the bias of her nature was not to thought, but to sympathy, yet was she so perfect in her own nature, as to meet intellectual persons by the fulness of her heart, warming them by her sentiments; believing, as she did, that by dealing nobly with all, all would show themselves noble.

I know that this Byzantine pile of chivalry or Fashion, which seems so fair and picturesque to those who look at the contemporary facts for science or for entertainment, is not equally pleasant to all spectators. The constitution of our society makes it a giant's castle to the ambitious youth who have not found their names enrolled in its Golden Book, and whom it has excluded from its coveted honors and privileges. They have yet to learn that its seeming grandeur is shadowy and relative: it is great by their allowance: its proudest gates will fly open at the approach of their courage and virtue. For the present distress, however, of those who are predisposed to suffer from the tyrannies of this caprice, there are easy remedies. To remove your residence a

couple of miles, or at most four, will commonly relieve the most extreme susceptibility. For, the advantages which fashion values, are plants which thrive in very confined localities, in a few streets, namely. Out of this precinct, they go for nothing; are of no use in the farm, in the forest, in the market, in war, in the nuptial society, in the literary or scientific circle, at sea, in friendship, in the heaven of thought or virtue.

But we have lingered long enough in these painted courts. The worth of the thing signified must vindicate our taste for the emblem. Everything that is called fashion and courtesy humbles itself before the cause and fountain of honor, creator of titles and dignities, namely, the heart of love. This is the royal blood, this the fire, which, in all countries and contingencies, will work after its kind, and conquer and expand all that approaches it. This gives new meanings to every fact. This impoverishes the rich, suffering no grandeur but its own. What *is* rich? Are you rich enough to help anybody? to succor the unfashionable and the eccentric? rich enough to make the Canadian in his wagon, the itinerant with his consul's paper which commends him "To the charitable," the swarthy Italian with his few broken words of English, the lame pauper hunted by overseers from town to town, even the poor insane or besotted wreck of man or woman, feel the noble exception of your presence and your house, from the general bleakness and stoniness;

to make such feel that they were greeted with a voice which made them both remember and hope? What is vulgar, but to refuse the claim on acute and conclusive reasons? What is gentle, but to allow it, and give their heart and yours one holiday from the national caution? Without the rich heart, wealth is an ugly beggar. The king of Schiraz could not afford to be so bountiful as the poor Osman who dwelt at his gate. Osman had a humanity so broad and deep, that although his speech was so bold and free with the Koran, as to disgust all the dervishes, yet was there never a poor outcast, eccentric, or insane man, some fool who had cut off his beard, or who had been mutilated under a vow, or had a pet madness in his brain, but fled at once to him,—that great heart lay there so sunny and hospitable in the centre of the country,—that it seemed as if the instinct of all sufferers drew them to his side. And the madness which he harbored, he did not share. Is not this to be rich? this only to be rightly rich?

But I shall hear without pain, that I play the courtier very ill, and talk of that which I do not well understand. It is easy to see, that what is called by distinction society and fashion, has good laws as well as bad, has much that is necessary, and much that is absurd. Too good for banning, and too bad for blessing, it reminds us of a tradition of the pagan mythology, in any attempt to settle its character. 'I overheard Jove, one day,' said

Silenus, 'talking of destroying the earth; he said, it had failed; they were all rogues and vixens, who went from bad to worse, as fast as the days succeeded each other. Minerva said, she hoped not; they were only ridiculous little creatures, with this odd circumstance, that they had a blur, or indeterminate aspect, seen far or seen near; if you called them bad, they would appear so; if you called them good, they would appear so; and there was no one person or action among them, which would not puzzle her owl, much more all Olympus, to know whether it was fundamentally bad or good.'